Feng Shui Fusion

First published in the United States in 2002 by
  Watson-Guptill Publications, a division of BPI Communications Inc.,
  770 Broadway, New York, NY 10003

Library of Congress Control Number: 2001097748

ISBN 0 8230 1658 7

This book was conceived, designed, and produced by The Ivy Press Ltd,
  The Old Candlemakers, West Street, Lewes, East Sussex, BN7 2NZ

Creative Director: Peter Bridgewater
Publisher: Sophie Collins
Editorial Director: Steve Luck
Design Manager: Tony Seddon
Project Editor: Georga Godwin
Designer and Illustrator: Molly Shields

Reproduction and Printing in China by
  Hong Kong Graphic and Printing Ltd

Feng Shui Fusion

Jane Butler-Biggs

Watson-Guptill

Contents

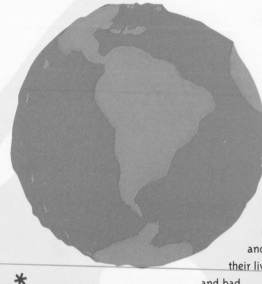

Introduction

This is a book about energy, the invisible source and motivator of all things. The Yogis in Asia call it Prana, the Chinese, chi, the Japanese call it Ki. For as long as people have been trying to make sense of their world and the part they play in it, they have attempted to describe, understand, and harness this quality of aliveness and spirit. People instinctively know that it is the quality of this energy, and its presence or absence in their surroundings and in their lives, that makes the difference between good times and bad.

✱

The natural flow of nature, the way the Earth and the universe exist so effortlessly and perfectly can be harnessed to bring harmony into your life.

So in a way too, this is a book about good times, and for me those times have always been when I have felt as though I was effortlessly going with the "flow," rather than against or at odds with it. These are the times when things just seem to fall into place and come my way, and I have enough vitality to really appreciate and get involved with each moment as it happens.

These are truly good times, and they have increasingly come my way as the result of living with an ongoing awareness of the power, purpose and role of energy, or chi, in my life. I think of this energy as chi because, for me, the bedrock of my understanding has been the Chinese perception and observation of the way in which this energy resides in our world. The description of this energy as yin and yang, and its breakdown into the five elements (Water, Wood, Fire, Earth, and Metal), has guided my understanding, and more importantly my practice, of this wonderful life source.

It was through my practice of Hatha Yoga that I first began to directly sense, or feel, the impact that chi has on our bodies, and it was my years spent as a yoga therapist and healer that enabled me to confirm, and recognize as real, the things I subsequently began to understand and appreciate when I began my study of Chinese philosophy. The Chinese teachings added structure and the wealth of knowledge, based on thousands of years of observation, analysis, and practice, to my growing experience of, and belief in, the role that "energy" plays in our lives, and particularly our sense of health and wellbeing.

Chi moves through the five elements, which are manifest in the yearly cycle of seasons. I discovered that, by developing a combination of practices, in tune with the natural rhythm and order of chi, the good times that we experience day to day, month to month, and year to year quite definitely and steadily increase.

Feng Shui Fusion is about sharing these discoveries, and empowering everyone who comes into contact with the realities that this book describes. By practicing a combination of Feng Shui and yoga, and paying attention to our emotional life and the way in which we feed our bodies—in tune with the changing rhythms of the five elements and the seasons—a wonderful fusion takes place, in which the whole becomes infinitely more than the sum of its parts.

Fusion is about the accessing and release of energy, so give the practices taught in the book to yourself, and begin by learning more about your own unique "energy."

*

The creative cycle: showing progression of season and element.

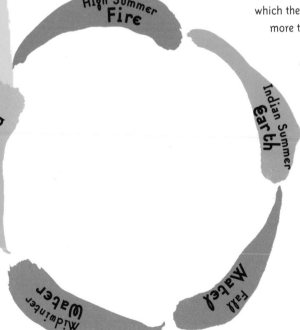

High Summer
Fire

Indian Summer
Earth

Spring
Wood

Fall
Water

Midwinter
Water

How To Use This Book

I wrote this book in one easy movement that took me from the stillness of the midwinter passages through the whole cycle. The persistence of spring and Wood, to the ignition and flowering of high summer and Fire. From the awesome gearing of the Earth phase, to the condensing drop through to fall, and the crystallisation and luminous movement of the Metal phase. Each section held me in its thrall and lent me its rhythm and unique quality as I wrote. The midwinter section alerted me to the moments of pause and space that were available to me once I knew how to look for them. The Fire section invited me write and live out my days with a light heart and an easy touch. As I neared the completion of the book a new presence began to emerge from the clutter, noise, and onward flow of my days, the presence of, and a sense of a connection to the whole. To the whole of the cycle, the whole of the planet, all of time to come, and time past. Each moment in time, each particle of space and place sits as part of a connection to every other, and to an amorphous being that is the whole—the sum of all the parts. Only as part of a whole can any moment or space exist, and it is in the extent of each moment's ability to connect to the whole that can be realized. It is in identifying the order of things and the ways in which they connect to each other and become part of the whole that

grew in me. As I wrote I came to realize that less can become more, that things can achieve their greater potential and that, what may have seemed vague, inaccessible or unattainable, can be made manifest.

Therefore, I suggest that you read *Feng Shui Fusion* as it was written—from the first section through to the last. Take your time, allow the ideas the book suggests, and the pictures it conjures to make a connection with you as they will, rather than as you imagine they ought. Suspend, for a time all cynicism and approach the book as a person with the permission (and time) to play and be delighted.

As the writer, hoping to ensure that some sort of fusion, some coming together and release of energy, takes place because of the existence of *Feng Shui Fusion*, I would ask one more thing of you. That you engage with the book, allowing it to stay alive while it is in your care. Please do it the honor of making numerous additions and inserts (or corrections and subtractions) Please take it with you from place to place so that it becomes wonderfully aged and connected to life's process, rather than leaving it to die a quiet death in impeccable condition on a bookshelf or as the proud adornment of some coffee table.

Better to be used as a work of reference, as a friend, and as a point of connection to all those other people across the world who are practicing the art of being alive.

1

Winter/Water

Introduction

In order to understand the nature of chi, we need to backtrack to the basics of yin and yang and five element theory. Chi has been observed to manifest differently as yin and yang, and this separation is further expressed in five ways, namely the five transformations or elements; Water, Wood, Fire, Earth, and Metal.

These elements each hold the seed of the one that follows, thus Water changes and transforms to Wood, Wood to Fire, Fire to Earth, Earth to Metal, and Metal to Water. So, the existence in time and space, (or place), of each element is dependent on its relationship to the whole. Each element is an expression of qualities that form part of a whole, in much the same way as spring follows winter, which has itself followed autumn. Each season, with all its special qualities and attributes, only makes sense when seen as part of the whole yearly cycle, and is valuable because of the special part it plays in the creation of the whole. As you work your way through this book, the chi of each element, as manifest in the seasons, will become familiar and easy for you to understand. The times relating to the fifth element, Earth energy, will also be covered.

The same is true of yin and yang, the two opposing qualities that change to balance one another in creating the whole. The quality of chi expressed by the element Water can be experienced in deep midwinter, or at midnight, when yin is at its strongest.

Yin is the chi of deep acceptance, of the power of receptivity, malleability, and the ability to hold still around movement. It is the moon cycle, the quality of energy that lifts up from the depths, dispersing and

Each season has its appointed time in the yearly cycle and its elemental expression, which bring harmony and spiritual balance.

diffusing to give safe space in which the creative impulse can take shape. The power of yin rests in this ability to flow and move as it is needed. It is sometimes explained as the feminine quality. The very source of its strength and power is its ability to be flexible, apparently vulnerable, cool, deep, and dark. Its pace is slow, its touch dense.

Our time spent with the Water element is a perfect place to begin our journey—in the context of this book, Water is an energetic type rather than the water that we drink, wash, and swim in, although the two do share some qualities. By being at one with this element we will learn how to be at one with ourselves. The perfect way to experience the quality of this chi is by experiencing to the full all the delights that winter has to offer us.

At the very mention of this word many of us will have already slightly tensed, turned away, shut off our keen interest and attention. Winter is a powerful, even fearful, time. Yet the power of this element during this time is invaluable if we are to realize our full potential as we move through the rest of the yearly cycle, enabling us to make our true potential manifest, moment by moment. Each season and each element is part of a whole both at any one moment, and over time.

*

By tapping into, and fully appreciating, the Water element we can realize our potential both during the wintertime and throughout the year. The winter season and Water element give us an opportunity to experience quiet and contemplation, preparing us for the exertions of the rest of the year.

In the winter most movement disappears from the Earth's surface. There is a natural movement away from outside activities, more time is spent indoors. Plant and animal life withdraw below the surface, plants and trees lie dormant. Life continues, but in a more peaceful different way than in the summer, or even the autumn.

Beyond this superficial transformation much deeper change is trying to assert itself. The world is yinising—moving toward the extreme of yin chi, therefore away from yang chi. The universal flow of chi is pulling all things inward, toward a space of stillness and deep toil. The absence of apparent movement is sometimes read as inactivity, in the same way as someone observing another person meditating may conclude that "nothing is happening to them." But much the same is happening in winter—if we allow it—as happens to an individual during meditation.

*

Winter is the time for contemplation, a time to gather our strength and renew our physical and spiritual energy—a time to prepare ourselves for the coming year.

Suggestions for Silence

- Observe and contemplate your own words
- Meditate in your winter garden
- Find time to reflect
- Enjoy your own company

The current trend is to oppose this process with all our might. Apparent inactivity is anathema to a society that holds the belief that creativity is something that expresses itself through action. The only stillness that many of us are familiar with is sleep, illness, or vegetating in front of the television. Creativity of thought is sanctioned, providing that there is a visible end product, but what of time to just sit and be, to allow what will be to be—even if that appears to be nothing?

I have learned from my yoga practice that it is the gaps in the silence that are often the most profoundly creative moments. The ability to accept stillness and all that it brings is a major part of the ability to be in balance in winter. Within this movement toward stillness and openness is the ability to lose control and accept our position as it is given to us, and at the moment of this acceptance to glimpse our own uniqueness, the thing that makes us completely and utterly different from every other being and thing. This first glimpse of one of the essential things that we can experience is vital if we are going to fulfill our potential by actually living this reality later in the year. So, acorns grow to oaks!

As I was writing this, I paused for a moment to turn to my garden and saw snow falling to the ground across the landscape of Downs and hills. It was in that moment of pause that I felt my own energy come to a rest and find its center before regrouping. It was that moment, and all the others like it that held the message of winter and of the Water element.

Feng Shui
Winter Living Space
The Exterior

Feng Shui, to help balance Water energy, or help us make the most of winter, has a lot to do with encouraging the yin quality of a space. Spaces that are predominantly yin tend to reflect this in their location, shape, structure, and design.

An extremely yin dwelling would be located on low-lying land, maybe even in a slight dip, surrounded by undulating hills with maybe a gently meandering shallow waterway making its way across the foreground. It would be surrounded by rounded deciduous trees, low scattered bushes and shrubs, and spatterings of multicolored wildflowers.

Its urban equivalent is happened upon around a turn in the road, unexpectedly placed among a cluster of ill-matched, though pleasing buildings. It is likely to be single story, with possibly one dormer window indicating a single upstairs room. A curving roof line might drop down to meet a wall softened by climbing plants. The whole might be reached via a meandering path to a porched doorway.

These yin dwellings seem to grow right out, and be embedded into, their yin locations. The energy is soft, sprawling, undirected, and accepting of all comers.

Once inside, movement itself may be negotiated through a series of arched gateways, inner and outer doors, the theme continues. The layout will tend to a lack of regimentation. The space is likely to sprawl before you, with one room leading from another, doors leading unexpectedly to further hallways, or even cupboards, steps leading up or down in twos and threes, and an abundance of low-lying windows with wide windowsills.

Yin energy lies low and relaxed, comfortable and cool—its emphasis is internal. During winter your home is the warm hearth you return to from the cold outside.

If you are already living in a house of this type, you will probably be very much at home with the dreamy poetic nature of yin and Water energy. You may even be in need of a little yangising! For the rest of us who need to become more familiar with the deep power of the qualities structures like these can bring us, we can look around our current space and ask ourselves just how much yin have we allowed into our lives. If the answer is not a lot, or none at all, then attending to and changing the exterior nature of our space is the gentlest and easiest way to begin to get in touch with that wonderful Water chi.

It is most important for us all to recognize what we are doing with our energy and why, and then we will understand what the effects of our actions are. If you have chosen to live on the top floor of an apartment building in the middle of an urban grid system, you maybe didn't feel that this was a good time to reflect and turn inward. That's fine, as long as you find a way to look after the store of inner strength that you have hopefully brought with you. You will almost certainly really value vacations spent in quiet places, where you can allow yourself to let go and return to your source.

Most of you reading this book will recognize some Watery elements in the style and location of your home, and can then make a considered choice about how to encourage and develop, or subtly redirect what you have currently chosen.

> The gentlest and easiest way to begin to get in touch with the easy peace of Water chi is to change the exterior nature of our space.

Exteriors

If up until now, you have always found it difficult to enjoy winter (except by escaping into somewhere else's summer!), you would do well to look with some care at the quality of the place in which you have chosen to live.

While all spaces should show a balance of all elements, a complete, or near absence of the yin Water features described, would suggest that you have concentrated in the past on using up your resources at the expense of spending any time building upon them. We learn from Chinese philosophy, and its practical application in Eastern-based medicine, that protecting our innate energy source is all-important. We should acknowledge that we are not invincible beings, who will be well-served by the "work hard, play even harder, party till late" lifestyle. Hard work, play, and partying have their place, but so does an awareness of our role in a greater dynamic. Like the rest of the natural world, we need to go to ground, consistently and periodically, to regroup our energy.

So let's go to ground in a place that's designed to support us while we rest, recuperate, and feed the seat of our creative energies. Take a mental stroll around the exterior of your space noticing any of the curving, flowing, or haphazard features that we talked about earlier. Exploit any opportunities to introduce some Watery features and soften that fast moving go-getting

Winter needn't be spent in wishing to be elsewhere—being at home supports our spiritual and physical energy.

space. The addition of climbing, rambling plants and garden landscaping to soften an angular building design (this can be a shallow peripheral patio, or the addition of a rounded flowerbed, or planters), would be one approach. Why have a regimented planting design at the front of your house, or a fence around the boundary when you could have a hedge?

This exercise is designed to wake your perceptions up to the correspondence between you and your lifestyle and the space that you have chosen to be in. If you alert your senses to the way that your environment reflects what you are doing with your life, you can begin to unpick its fabric and redesign according to your current needs.

In the U.K. there is a large amount of Victorian housing stock. These houses were built at a time when the work ethic was newly established, and the self was held in check lest the unexpected latent creative spirit rear its ugly head and spoil the timetable, or worse, the collectively imposed moral order. The houses are set out in tight little rows and are as upright and predictable in their design as their occupants. A very common problem for people calling me out on consultations in these houses is the inability to relax there, the difficulty of finding creativity and fluidity within them.

So what can you do if you live in a structure like this? The first step is to recognize why you were attracted to the space. Being prepared to take responsibility for the position you find yourself in at any time is a key to working out what you want to do next. Acknowledge and be grateful for what the space has already given, or taught, you, and then decide whether or not you want to move to a different position in your life.

The achievement of balance in our lives is a healthy goal so, having done all we can to soften the exterior of our living space, we will now turn our attention to providing harmony inside.

*

Softening the exterior structures of your home could be the first step to welcoming the Water element into your space and your life. Any property no matter how seemingly high tech or rigid can be softened through landscaping and planting.

Moving Inside

Spending time, perhaps sometimes alone, taking your ease in your home, does not mean installing yourself on the coziest couch sometime in late autumn and rarely moving until the first dawning of spring. Dozing in a semiconscious state in front of a television screen is not the sort of rest and stillness that will do anything much at all to repair your depleted Water chi. Essential to generating the kind of regeneration you need is the concept of movement or flow.

One of the first practical steps that you can take to help support your Water energy is to sort out both the quality and patterns of your sleep. Seriously consider getting yourself to a position where as much regular sleep, during the hours of darkness, as possible can be yours. Consider this as the most essential gift that you can give yourself as you begin your program of rejuvenation.

With this in mind take yourself (in your mind, or body) to the place, which you usually sleep. This needs to be a place specifically designed to sleep in—I have been amazed to find how many people attempt to find good quality sleep in a room full of computers, gym equipment, televisions, or other assorted items, some of which are at complete odds with rest and sleep. Step one; consider the location of this room within the house. Does the place that you are sleeping in feel the safest, calmest, most yin part of your home? Is it the most appropriate location for your position in the family? In other words are you, for instance, the parent of four young children attempting to sleep in a ground floor extension, while they sleep in converted attic rooms? You may find it more relaxing to bring the sleeping arrangements onto one level. Are you occupying a room closest to the front door because it was the only place the removal company could put your bed? The little room upstairs may really be the place for you to dream in.

You may end up changing all the sleeping arrangements in the house, more than once, before you settle with an

When sleeping physical and mental energies are regenerated. Allow yourself the time and space to fully appreciate this potential.

arrangement that brings out the best for everyone. Don't forget that, particularly in a growing family, people's needs change, so that you will need to reassess the situation from time to time.

No one needs to sleep in a place that does not support their own unique needs. Addressing our own unique needs and desires will feed us in a way that no amount of "correct Feng Shui" or healthy eating will. So let's start as we mean to go on, here in the beginning of the cycle. Good Feng Shui is Feng Shui that makes us feel good—not that makes our partner, or our friend, or an expert feel good... If we are to take responsibility for becoming more conscious of our own chi, then we owe it to ourselves to keep on asking "Does this feel good to me?"

*

Choosing the right rooms for all your family to sleep in will provide each of them with the perfect place to recover from the day's exertions, and a safe place from which to start their daily journey. Helping each family member to structure their room to suit their individual needs will make each person more aware and appreciative of their own energy.

So back in the bedroom, try walking all around the room to find out where you would get the best quality rest. Be prepared to end up moving your bed to a very unexpected spot. While you're thinking about moving your bed, take a good look at it. Is it really "your" bed or does it in fact hold some one else's energy? Is it a place that will allow you to feel safe, supported, and calm while you rest? Extend that line of questioning to other pieces of furniture in the room. The range of gilt mirrored wardrobes opposite your bed may begin speaking volumes to you in reply! So may the angular shelving racks or red striped blinds at the window, or some tiny unexpected object full of memories of a time of upset and rage.

Why not be kind to your self and create a haven of peace, clarity, and warmth to sleep in this winter?

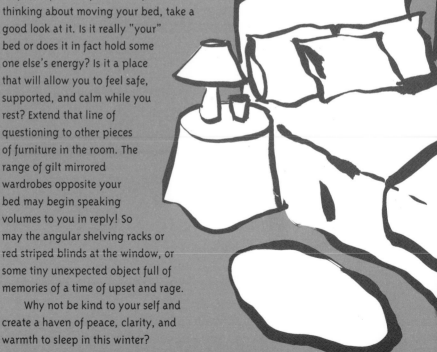

More interiors

What about the rest of your living space? A grand tour, starting at the front door, and neglecting no area—however small and seemingly insignificant—will allow you to begin the process of tuning in to the Water chi that flows through your space.

Notice, first, the layout of your home. As you stand at the front door, does it open before you horizontally, meandering and haphazard? Does the hallway run from front to back with rooms off at regular intervals? Is the design obvious and predictable, or do doors open unexpectedly on to rooms, that seem to contain further hidden mysteries? Try and recall the first time you saw the space, or ask a friend's opinion. This will help you to assess the true nature of your space. You are trying to feel how yin the space already is, and therefore what sort of effort you will have to make to soften it.

Taking a closer look at some key rooms will prove useful in trying to provide yourself with a wonderful space to dive into this winter. Every home should have at least one room that is designed specifically to relax in. Classically, this would be a north-facing room, but having been brought up in a chilly climate, I personally would break this rule every time and go for a sunny south-facing room where I could curl up and bask in stolen sunshine.

It's important to take time to list the ingredients that add up to a relaxing space for you personally—a great long distance view out of a picture window will help to make you feel

*

Create small individually comfortable spaces within each room, half hidden like gifts to yourself—places to sit and be still.

Some basic yin ingredients to slow down any space are:

- good quality soft furnishings in cool blues or hushed and muted tones
- rounded, low sofas
- layers of drapes at windows
- layered floor coverings (polished wood softened with wonderful dense rugs)
- beautiful visuals everywhere to inspire creative dreamtime

dreamy and light, or a cozy nook with a pretty little draped window may be what you need to feel safe and relaxed. Everyone needs different things to bring out their poetry.

At this point I would like to alert every one of you to the potential hazards of "claggy" soft furnishing! This includes all upholstered items that have absorbed all sorts of stress, strain, and angst, from their sometimes numerous owners, and have never been properly cleared. Clearing these items involves removing cushions and any covers possible and physically cleaning them, if possible in the fresh air, and with movement of wind or manually beating and shaking them. All remaining parts should be moved out of their location, and cleaned in any way possible. If everything fails to create a beautiful, sweet-smelling, bright-feeling piece of furniture, then you are better to move it out of your space forever, even if this means sitting on the floor with the aid of rugs and cushions! This is extreme, but essential work, if your wintertime is to be anything but a descent into the dull boredom of waiting for spring.

Once you have cleaned and cleared all your soft furnishings, turn your attention to setting up your space specifically for winter. The furniture arrangement that may have been ideal for the long summer days may not suit your needs now that your attention has turned to building up your store of intrinsic energy. Consider creating nestlike arrangements for seating, with comfort high on your list of priorities. Once you have set up a series of wonderful places to be, sit down in them and check out the view from each location. What meets your eye? Inspiration, regeneration, creativity are all key words here. Keep rearranging until you have at least a couple of locations, not necessarily in the same room, that fit the bill.

Just as people put on winter clothing to suit the weather so a home needs to adopt a winter arrangement to provide warmth and comfort during the long nights ahead. Creating soft cozy warmth is the key, but clearing allows stale energy to leave enabling us to move on to the year ahead.

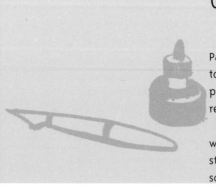

Work Space

Part of the energy package that says "Water" is the concept of labor or toil, meaning that slow type of conscientious, consistent work, that often provides the foundation for projects destined to soar, or bring in great results, later in the year.

The approach of winter is the time when students are called back to work, and really need to get their heads down and begin some serious study. Winter is a good time to settle down and spend time negotiating some of the more daunting tasks that need a certain amount of doggedness.

So how do you set up your work space to support this part of your work process? How much you can actually do to your environment will be different for everyone, but even people who feel that they have almost no control over their workspace will be able to make changes that will make a difference to the way that they feel about their space.

As we spend so much time at work it is important that our work space support us emotionally.

Start by taking an objective look at your workspace. See how much room for maneuver you have. It may be more than you think. Your boss may actually be pleased that your are committed enough to be taking an interest in the space and may really welcome your input.

If you work from home, or can have full control over your workplace design, you may want to approach this space in a similar way to the way in which you approached your living space. Obviously, while you are working you need to be more alert and concentrated than while you are at leisure, but the same principles apply. Aim to create a warm comfortable space where you could happily spend long periods of time if necessary.

Concentrate on arranging your furniture so that your back is supported by proximity to a wall. Sitting with your back facing a door, or in the line

> Aim to create a warm comfortable space where you could happily spend long periods of time if necessary.

of passing people traffic is not going to support you. If you cannot do this, a heavy jacket placed on the back of your chair will help.

Notice what is in your line of vision while you are working, and if you spend long periods sitting at a screen provide yourself with an inspiring image—as far distant as space allows—on which to rest your eyes.

When I am out consulting in work locations, I often spend time working on ways to remedy noise pollution. The stress of working in a space that is noisier than you would like it to be can be extremely wearing, and it is really worth spending time investigating all the ways to reduce this very real pain. Reorienting work stations can reduce noise considerably; acoustic screens are great if there are the resources to introduce these. Otherwise introducing any softer fabric into the make-up of the space can help considerably by absorbing the unwanted distraction.

Beyond these structural changes to the space, it is possible to introduce an element of comfort into an environment quite simply by rechoosing the paraphernalia with which you surround yourself. Choose softer gentler items, denser textures, a more accessible layout, or simply iron out minor irritations such as constantly having to reach past an angular desk end to use the wastepaper basket.

Attention to detail can often turn a hostile work environment into a friendly one, it's just a matter of taking time out to consider how your space is making you feel, and therefore affecting your performance at work.

When creating a balanced work space be aware of the very real seemingly minor irritations— reducing these can help us not just when we're at work, but the reduction of stress here will have a considerable effect on other areas of our lives. It is important that we create spaces that make us feel safe and supported—just as we do at home.

Emotional Wellbeing
Learn about Yourself

Having spent some time looking at the Feng Shui of your space, you will have begun to get some ideas about how at ease you are with the unique qualities of Water energy. Looking at the exterior of your house, and the way it sits in its location, will have begun to tell you a story about yourself, if you're willing to listen. If you approach a situation with a head already full of ideas about what you're expecting to find, and a heart even more sure that you have done everything wrong, then you are sure to find a lot of the very thing you expected. Approach a situation with fear, and you will find fear exists there; approach it with a light heart and this will be reflected back. So the way in which you begin to look, and sense, is all-important. Whenever I go out on a consultation, to work with a space, an individual, or even a company, I aim to carry the same things with me; an open mind, an open heart, an intuitive alertness, and above all a quality of unconditional acceptance and love. I simply would not approach healing work in any other way!

So, now that you are going to begin to look more closely at your own space, I would suggest that you "put out" an intention to let go of all the rigidity of thought and feeling that might get in the way of your listening well to the energetics of yourself and your space. Intentions are incredibly powerful, great tools that can help you in the ongoing way in which you create your life. Beyond this, if you meet your findings from a position of acceptance and compassion, then more

Our surroundings are a reflection of ourselves, so it is doubly important to take some time and reflect upon the spaces we create, what they show about us and how we would like them to change and expand.

You may have found yourself living in the midst of a great sea, which could explain why you've been feeling completely overwhelmed by life lately.

and more will be revealed to you. Many of us will quite happily give to others what we hold back from ourselves—perhaps the first message here is simply to be kind to oneself.

You may have found that you are living in a place that has a wonderful contribution from the Water element ingredients already discussed. Whatever you have concluded, everyone will have been able to find something in their space that felt fluid and calming. You may have found yourself living in the midst of a great sea, which could explain why you've been feeling completely overwhelmed by life lately. Whichever position is yours, I hope that you have been able to introduce some sense of balance into your space by encouraging changes to your design, decor, and placement.

Already during this process you will almost certainly have encountered certain emotional responses to your findings. So you have already discovered the connection between your external living space and your inner emotional space. After all, if there were no connection, then Feng Shui wouldn't be a Healing Art at all!

Moving from External to Internal space

As you look at your own space, your findings may confirm things that you already knew about yourself. Maybe you were always really good at nurturing yourself at the deepest level, and this is reflected by a space that has a wonderful acceptance of yin energy in its very design, which you have naturally supported with additions of furnishings and color. During the course of the book we will get used to looking at the Feng Shui, or the energetic qualities of our spaces, as a way of finding out more about what we need to bring our lives into balance. At first, this way of approaching our emotional wellbeing may seem a little labored and self-conscious, but as you practice more and more, as when learning any new skill, the process becomes increasingly integrated into your everyday life.

You have begun to support your own inner Water energy by making changes around and inside your home, and a process will already have begun that will involve that part of your emotional life which is largely related to Water chi. Now may be a good time to find one of those wonderful safe and calming spaces that you have created and simply spend some time reflecting on what has happened since you began your Feng Shui practice.

Take time to acknowledge the emotions that you may have felt since starting to look at the chi of your space. You may even have felt a lot while reading the text and looking at the pictures. The emotions that we present to ourselves often surface in layers, and therefore need that unhurried accepting Water chi to be truly felt. Often the initial emotion is buried under a rather fine disguise of boredom, tiredness, irritation, or even the sudden need to go and eat, or do anything but feel. I have got many of my most hated chores done while trying to avoid feeling an uncomfortable emotion!

This is why staying alert for a time that you have agreed with yourself and refusing to become involved in a diversionary tactic can be so powerful in allowing feelings to surface. If you start to see feelings, however

Examining your surroundings to discover yourself is a skill that takes practice, but with time it becomes second nature and is a valuable tool to understanding and caring for yourself.

Developing your Water chi will allow you to relax and care for yourself. It will bring harmony into your life, balancing the hectic modern day lifestyle. Water chi allows your emotions to surface and be felt in a much deeper way, strengthening your understanding of your own needs, and, through a deeper understanding of others, it will enhance your relationships.

uncomfortable, as your greatest allies, life will really begin to move on for you. We all experience sensation in the body to alert us to potential danger, and it's the same with the emotional body. If things are going wrong for us surely we need to know about it so that we can take appropriate action. By practicing the art of allowing yourself to have feelings, you will be strengthening your Water chi, which will effect your whole body, mind, and spirit.

In Chinese medicine the kidneys, bladder function, brain, and skeletal structure are all supported by Water chi, so working to balance your Water chi via your emotions will be incredibly transforming for your whole self. This connection between spaces is fundamental to Chinese philosophy and medicine, to treat the body is to treat the mind, to heal your emotional life is to make well your whole body and being.

Water Chi Emotions

The internal organs affected by Water chi are seen to have a more complex and far-reaching role within the body than is usual in some types of Western medicine. Thus a relationship between kidney energy, as a storehouse for an individual's inherited health, and their ability to develop, mature, and become fertile in order to reproduce and continue the energetic line, is assumed. The kidney function is seen to reflect the source of vitality, constitutional reserve, and ongoing ability to sustain and promote life. Some of the Feng Shui adjustments that we have made to our living space will allow us to support and nurture this deep-seated, profound source of all our energies. The connection between kidney or Water chi and the survival of the gene pool is manifest on the emotional level as an ability to harness the power, both of thought and emotion, to keep oneself alive and out of danger.

The brain and its workings are also seen to be governed by Water chi. Ongoing thought patterns concerned

The emotions associated with Water chi are very powerful—they exist at the core of our beings and our need to survive.

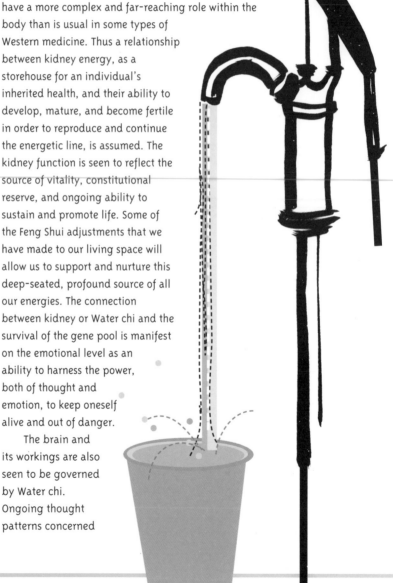

The connection between kidney or Water chi and the survival of the gene pool is manifest on the emotional level as an ability to harness the power, both of thought and emotion, to keep oneself alive and out of danger.

with survival promote associated beliefs, such as the profound awareness of the importance of our continuing existence, our states of separateness from and connection to people around us, our deep connection to the past and the future, and the unique contribution it is incumbent on each one of us to make to the totality of the whole. Water chi can give rise to overwhelming and all-pervasive emotions and it is important that we keep these feelings moving.

Often when experiencing Water emotions we find ourselves using "watery images" and terms. People often express a water imbalance by saying things like "I feel as though I'm drowning," "I just felt frozen to the spot," "nothing seems to be flowing right." People's emotions become "dammed up," "dried out," or they feel "swept away." These feelings of being overwhelmed by life, or frozen (sometimes described as feeling paralyzed, unable to act at all), are indications of Water chi imbalance. Creating a balance of chi in your environment is the first step toward rectifying this imbalance.

Give time to tuning in to these feelings and allow their source to become a positive creative force in your life. After all, at their source is the fundamental desire to survive, so with a little bit of understanding and re-patterning these feelings could support you in the simple business of living life to the fullest.

Taking Action

Acknowledgment and acceptance of your emotions is vital when balancing your chi to bring spiritual harmony.

Here is something that you can do in order to listen to the quality of your own Water chi. Please remember that what you bring to this exercise will have a bearing on what you receive. Look at this series of questions and allow yourself some time to feel the answer to each one surfacing. Take care to find the perfect answer to each question, using only three or four words that express the exact energy of your response.

- How often do you feel adventurous?
- How much time do you spend anticipating life's pitfalls?
- When did you last feel safe?
- Are you expecting a secure future?
- Do you feel a certain amount of anxiety most of the time?

Sometimes the answer that comes to mind will make you feel pleased and happy, other times it may come as something of a shock, or moment of realization that can make you feel sad, angry, or despondent, other times the answer given will be all too familiar and a sense of boredom and frustration may creep in.

Whatever your response to these questions, the way you react is all-important in the process. Aim to accept each response in an equally loving and nonjudgmental way. Acknowledging feelings, both good and bad, allows your own chi to deal effectively with them.

This way of working with emotional responses is a powerful tool that all healers can, and often do, use. It is the simple practice of witnessing. It requires no comprehension, analysis, or action, simply loving acceptance and acknowledgment. Witnessing is an incredibly powerful part of the healing process that you can give to yourself every time you are working to balance your own chi.

The five questions above share a common theme. They all tap in to the role fear plays in your life. Feeling fearful, of the present, future, or the past, trying to anticipate and protect yourself from fearful situations, or trying to blot out the memory of times when you haven't been able to protect

yourself, can occupy large amounts of your energy and time, leading you to develop all sorts of strange defense mechanisms, designed to protect you from danger, but actually protecting you from life itself. The survival instinct goes into overdrive.

The problem is that the more you operate from a fear-based position, the further you throw your kidney energy out of balance, and drive down your reserve of the very chi that you were trying to protect. You can heal this pattern by simply understanding what is going on, identifying the fear-based feelings and actions in all their many disguises, and outing them (calling them by their name), and by working with the body (see pages 36—45) to release old memories and patterns on a cellular level.

Simple but effective!

More action with Water Emotions

How easily fear is turned into courage, when we "feel the fear and do it anyway." Remember also that an extreme inability to feel fear is seen as an indication of an imbalance. So with all other emotions, every perceived negative is really only the flipside of a positive.

With that in mind, let's explore some other feelings that may hover around the wintery you! Take time to read one by one through this list of statements, simply witnessing your response to each one:

- My past was great, and I feel very happy to take all my experiences with me into the future.
- I seem to do things very differently from everyone else, but that's what I love about myself.
- I know that I had such a fantastic start in life, that everything else will go well.
- Being alone, or being in a group is equally comfortable for me, and always has been really.
- I can't wait to see what happens next in my life!

All these statements may sit well with you, in which case, smile and turn over. For the rest of us, let's look at the emotions and mind sets that they are tapping into.

Balanced Water chi allows us to grow and develop through every stage of our life simply and appropriately. But, sometimes you can find yourself getting stuck at one stage or another, simply unable to proceed. Physically our bodies may not flow from one time to another, causing symptoms to do with our sexuality, fertility, menstruation, or menopause. Children may appear to develop or mature late.

All these may be due to Water chi imbalance, and, in my experience of working with many people over the years, can be helped, sometimes overcome, by looking at issues concerning your own origins, and your own deep-seated feelings about what might happen if you proceed to the next stage in your life. Very often you need to get back in touch with your own source, and understand the impact it has had on your life before you can move on.

Many years ago a young woman was sent to me by her doctor; her reproductive system was, frankly, a mess and she was unable to conceive the child she longed for. We started immediately on a program of yoga asanas designed to open her body up and revitalize it. Within a couple of weeks of her seeing me, she began to chat about what was happening to her during her yoga practice. Great feelings of sadness and loss were surfacing and a lot of her time with me was spent releasing huge amounts of grief and crying, although by her own admission she was a generally cheerful person. As I continued to witness her emotional state, she began to talk to me quite out of the blue about her own beginnings. Although she had had a happy childhood, it transpired that her own mother had died giving birth to her, an event which she had rarely considered, and had never spoken about to her father, or the aunt who raised her. As our work continued she slowly wove her way back to the depth of her feelings about the nature of womanhood and being a mother. A short time after we stopped working together she sent me a card announcing the birth of her baby daughter.

We each have our own story, and each have a right moment to tell it. The statements above may trigger your own feelings about being part of life's process, about the ways in which you deal with being unique, and the ways in which you listen to your feelings and are happy to accept and learn from them.

*

Our sense of our own uniqueness, our sense of holding our being entirety within ourselves, can be a joy. It can become our way to connect with others.

Yoga
Introduction

I began my practice of Hatha Yoga over 20 years ago, when for many people it was a kind of Eastern acrobatics, a test of the body's strength and agility. The yogis performed alarming feats and, with the best of intentions, encouraged us students to follow in their paths. Having arrived at yoga from a strict dance background, I found all of this familiar, and enjoyed putting my body through its paces in this new arena. It came of something of a surprise therefore, when, after a lapse of some months, I joined a new class to find something quite different, and certainly altogether more profound going on.

I was introduced to a type of yoga that I have been practicing, teaching, and using as a fundamental tool in my life and my healing work ever since. The cornerstones of this way of practicing were:

Yoga is much more than a test of physical strength—practicing it brings emotional strength.

TRUST in the desire and ability of our bodies to become strong and open without the need of force or striving.

ACCEPTANCE in the ability of the ground to support and nourish the body during this process.

REALIZATION that our breath is our greatest ally throughout our practice.

GENEROSITY of spirit, as we give ourselves to each asana in an attitude of listening to our bodies' needs from a position of humility.

It was a way of practicing that was absolutely noncompetitive, there was no pressure to achieve a final pose, the whole atmosphere in the class was one of support and enjoyment.

Practicing in this way began to transform my body, and my emotional life in a way that I could hardly have hoped for, and I have continued to develop this style of yoga over the years into the form that you will be learning in the pages of this book. I propose for you a few guidelines:

Your yoga practice should be simple and individual—once you have mastered the basics your body is its own teacher. Over time yoga will become an integral part of your life to be practiced whenever your body needs it.

- During your practice, always listen to your own body's needs, never push it to do things that go against its natural instinct.
- If you are currently working with other healthcare professionals, discuss your yoga practice with them.
- You will need a few simple tools; some nonslip floor space, some clear wall space, and possibly, a selection of cushions, or a folded rug, to support your body in some of the floor-based postures.

The simplicity of these requirements is important, and an intrinsic part of this style of yoga, it will mean that you can take your yoga practice with you wherever you go. You will be able to sit in parks, on beaches, in hotel rooms, even quiet corners of airports, and enjoy the benefits that your yoga will give to you. It is often when your normal routine is disrupted and you are away from home that you, (and your body) will need yoga the most, so it is important that it can become a portable usable asset in your life, not some separate event that you participate in once a week under the specific direction of an "expert."

You can become your own teacher, using this book as a springboard, turning to the classic texts, or joining classes to augment and support the things you already have come to know about your own body and its unique needs.

Supine Kona Asana

The asanas (postures) that we will be looking at for the winter section of the book will all help to balance your Water Chi. I sometimes refer to yoga postures as "asanas," and now is a good time to explain why. The beautiful Sanskrit word *asana* holds within it the meanings, "seat," or "beginning place," or "base" (if we look at all the connotations of the English words seat or base, we will see that this is not so different in our language). So this word implies a grounded and strong location, or position, which serves as a source, or a beginning point, from which to develop. All these ideas are held in the word asana, so it is a powerful way of bringing a certain quality of energy to a posture

In this first asana we are looking to open the hips while the back is resting fully supported by its position against the ground. This is a wonderfully safe starting position for any of your yoga practice, or something to do if you are feeling anxious or fearful. This asana acts as an affirmation of your right to be alive and survive at the most fundamental level.

To arrive in this position;

1. lie down on the ground with your legs toward the wall

2. roll onto your side

3. curl your legs up and shuffle toward the wall until your bottom is in direct contact with the wall.

4. Bring your legs straight up against the wall, being careful to keep your bottom in contact with the wall.

Enjoy the sensation of support for your back, the contact with the ground, while your legs are stretching up toward the ceiling. Accept the sensation of stretching in the back of your legs, it is nothing to worry about. As time goes on, you will find it easier and easier to straighten your legs. However, the aim is to release your legs into the stretch, always keeping your hips and the whole length of your spine, including the back of your neck right up to the base of your skull, relaxed and heavy against the ground.

At first rest your arms wherever they feel most comfortable, but as you progress in your practice, you may wish to take your arms, first out to the sides (palms of your hands upturned), and eventually to a position resting

Feel the contact of the wall against the length of your legs, supporting them and drawing them upward, before allowing them to release away as your hips and back settle further into the ground.

above your head, (palms remain upturned throughout). Your arms should rest against the floor and not hover in the air.

Breathe naturally in through your nose, but exhale through a soft, relaxed, slightly open mouth. Maintain this way of breathing throughout the posture. You are now ready to proceed to the next part of the asana.

Next time you breathe out allow your legs to open into a V-shape, still keeping contact between your bottom and the wall, aiming to keep your legs relatively straight. You can move your legs in and out of this position as many times as you want to, always moving slowly, with the out-breath.

The eventual aim of the asana is to rest for some minutes with legs apart against the wall while breathing easily and relaxing the back, neck, shoulders, and arms completely. You should feel your hips opening, your legs and arms stretching, and the whole length of your spine, including your neck, supported by the floor.

Supine Twist

This posture is a wonderfully safe twist that will begin to open and tone the muscles of your back, while allowing you to explore the feelings held in the heart center at the front and back of the body. As your spine creates a beautiful spiral against the safety of the ground, your heart can open, and your breath can move to carry fresh chi through your whole being. As a bonus, the asana will also help move your hips in preparation for the more extreme asanas to come.

Allow your spine to rotate and your shoulders to open as you journey in this beautiful asana.

You can move into this asana straight from the one on the previous page, one movement flowing out of the other. Remain with your hips firmly against the wall, and your back resting against the ground. Establish your breath before you begin the pose, letting it move through the posture like a river. Remember that for this Water series of postures we will continue to breathe naturally and easily in through the nose, allowing the breath to leave our bodies, through a relaxed mouth.

To move in to the posture:

1. allow your folded legs to slide down onto your chest. The weight of your folded legs will begin to open your lower back and hips.

2. open your arms against the ground (palms upturned), as though you were flying.

3. rest here, allowing your body to open with your breath, while you completely surrender the weight of your body to the ground.

4. enjoy a really deep breath, and as you slowly and fluidly exhale, rotate your head to look away from your legs so that one ear turns toward the ground, and the other lifts toward the sky.

5. release any tension that has crept into your shoulders at this point, before taking another full breath in, and allowing your "joined together" knees to fall to the other side of your body, so that your spine forms a spiral and your chest is opening.

Your feet will stay in contact with the wall throughout.

If this movement sends your arm flying skyward, or if it pull or jars your body, try piling up some of your cushions under your legs or arm to support them.

If your knees do not touch the ground you may wish to place a folded rug or cushion under your knees so that you can relax in this asana.

Should you find this movement an absolute joy, and want to expand it, you could straighten your legs, slowly, on an exhalation and eventually catch your toes in your hand.

You should aim to be able to stay in the posture for a couple of minutes enjoying a feeling of unwinding, before coming back to the center ready to repeat the asana on the other side.

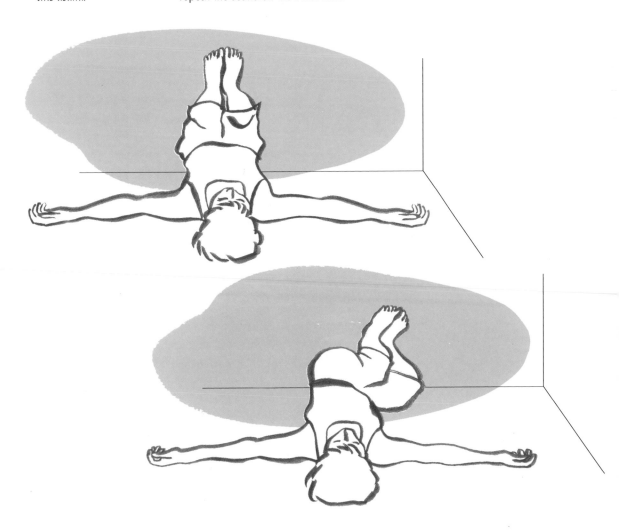

Baddha konasana

For this pose you can either move away from the wall, or stay close by, using the wall to support the whole of your spine. This asana makes the shape of a great open angle with the hips and legs, but with all the chi held inward by the binding of the angle at the soles of the feet. The stillness of the torso lifts clear out of the pelvis and up toward the sky. This is the perfect Water pose.

To arrive in this posture, begin with your back straight against the wall, and draw the soles of your feet together. People vary enormously as to what happens to their knees at this point; it doesn't matter what is happening to them as long as they don't feel unduly pulled or stressed. A way to find out what your own body needs at this point is to play with the pose, drawing your feet closer to, or further from, your groins. You are aiming to feel a sensation of stretching and opening in your hips and along your legs. If your back has remained effortlessly straight throughout, you may wish to move away from the wall, continuing in the center of the room, with your spine still lifting easily and smoothly skyward. As you sit in this position, you need to be very aware of your spine and avoid the desire to collapse or slouch.

Use your attention on your breath to stay alert and open, lifting your spine upward out of your hips, as you enjoy a complete inhalation. As you exhale, be aware of your shoulder line, and shoulder blades dropping, as they shed tension. Right at the end of your exhalation allow a feeling of the ground moving up to meet your body and take its weight downward.

Allow your hips and legs to feel whatever they need to feel as their own story unfolds, helping them to release by keeping your jaw relaxed and your mouth gently open.

The position of your arms will add an interesting new dimension to the pose. Begin with the backs of your hands resting on your legs close to your knees, or with your hands folded in your lap. Having spent what feels like a long time (and this will be different for everyone) in this position, feel the

The affirmation for this asana is "I grow from a place of stillness."

*

*As your hips open and
your spine lifts skyward,
allow yourself a smile.*

impact on your chi when you slowly move your
arms to stretch them above your head. As
you do this be sure to leave the base of your
body undisturbed, and keep that river
that is your breath flowing
unfalteringly through your
body. Keep breathing in
through a relaxed nose,
and out through
your mouth.

Konasana

The affirmation for this asana is "I am perfect just the way I am."

The asana that completes this cycle take us back to an acknowledgment of the very first posture, but fittingly, from a new perspective. I call this "the mighty Konsana," and you will understand why when you make your first journey with it! This asana will become your great friend and ally, just as long as you don't take your self too seriously while you spend time with it.

As with the previous asana, you may begin supported by the wall, moving away on those days when your spine lifts effortlessly out of your hips in a fluid movement up toward the sky. It is a huge and, potentially, extremely powerful, liberating stretch, but you will get nothing but misery from it if you see it as a way of testing your body, or a measure of your ability to achieve some personal goal.

1.   simply arrive in a seated position with your legs stretched out at an angle before you. Your back remains straight throughout its length.

2.   breathe in through a relaxed nose and out through a relaxed mouth, as before.

3.   be aware of your breath without trying to influence it in any way.

4.   the angle of your legs, as they are placed before you, will widen as you gain confidence and ease with this asana.

At first concentrate on keeping your spine lifted, your legs and hips completely relaxed and free of tension, and your face equally relaxed. It is an interesting fact that rather then letting go of tension, many of us find it easier to simply move it to a place of lesser resistance, hence the amount of tension that can end up in the shoulders, neck, or face when working to release other parts of the body. Aim instead to learn to use the ground as a place to release tension into. Consciously send the tension down through the body and beyond, deep into the ground, allowing your body to open and release around your breath.

If you feel very happy with this asana, a beautiful way to progress is to begin to pivot your torso forward, moving toward a time when your torso

Play with this asana until your legs give their weight to the ground and your hips are set free. Watch that your knees and the tops of your feet face skyward.

and arms are stretched out on the floor. This, however, is definitely a movement to aspire to, or a direction to follow. If you do try this, remember that your legs and hips will open happily and healthily with the movement beginning in your hips, not by curving your spine.

On the other hand, you could find a comfortable position by placing a stack of cushions on the floor in front of you and resting forward, either with hands, elbows, or your torso on the cushions. When resting in this way, allow the spine to curve gently and drop your head forward with the momentum of the stretch, and above all don't forget to breathe!

Food

What feeds you?

Before you read any more, take time to pause, and to consider carefully that question. Notice that it raises a range of issues. Most of us know what we like to eat, know what we usually eat, know, above all, what we think we ought to be eating. Where food is concerned we are the great experts. We know what disagrees with us, what we think will make us fat, what will make us strong, what makes us feel guilty, sad, or bad, what we eat in private, and what we like to be seen eating. The food we chose to eat becomes part of our image of ourselves, the way we feel about ourselves, and judge ourselves. We spend hours thinking about what we have just eaten, might eat later, or what we are trying to eat or not to eat right now. We spend days wondering if what we are eating is doing us good, or causing any number of symptoms that we are experiencing. But most of us are only seeing a very small and selective part of the total food picture.

To find out what your current position relating to food is, look at this list of simple questions and aim to answer them equally simply:

- What food would feed you well today?
- How would you like that food to make you feel?
- What food would you be able, and likely, to eat today?
- How will that food make you feel?
- What action can you take today that will make you happier about the answers that you have given?

The way you have answered, or been unable to answer, will already have told you a lot about your own relationship with food today. The way we feed ourselves is important—in order for food to be going right to our source, and feeding the storehouse of our kidney chi, it must be feeding us on a whole series of levels. In order to take the food into our bodies and be fed at the deepest level we need to really look at our relationship, not only to the food we actually eat on a day-to-day basis, but to the whole idea of feeding ourselves through eating.

If you have not chosen to commit to being fully alive, then it will be very difficult for you to allow yourself to be fed, by yourself or by anyone else. Your preparedness to feed yourself to the best of your abilities is directly related to your feeling about being alive in the first place. Are you eating to increase your vitality, vigor, and longevity, or for some other reasons altogether? You could be eating to reduce your feeling of being alive, to feel less, be able to do less, feel more sleepy, comforted, and dull. This may be because you are not yet enjoying the business of being alive!

Food is not just about physical sustenance—eaten the Feng Shui way, food is about feeding our emotional and spiritual lifeforce.

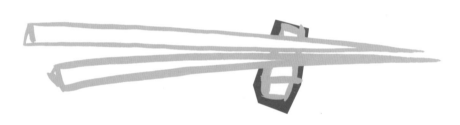

The Emotional Connection

We have already talked about learning to experience a range of feelings without fear. As we develop an ability to use our feelings as tools to help us make decisions about our lives, we will find ourselves increasingly seeking out the ability to feel more alive and less dull, semiconscious, confused, or stuck in our lives. As this process continues, we may find that our attitude to food, and our actual eating habits change, without any conscious effort at all. Feelings of self-worth, fulfillment, the ability to find self-expression and be acknowledged and "seen" for who we are, will make us feel happier, and more committed to the business of being alive. Ways of eating that will feed us at the deepest, the Water chi, level will follow on quite naturally. Deal with your emotional life, and food and nourishment will fall into place.

If you continue to use food in a way that you are not happy with, one way to sort out the connection between your eating and your emotions, (or the way you feel about your life), is to use your food intake to lead you to the emotional work that you need to do. Having done that you can also look at direct ways in which you can alter your eating to feed your Water chi, but it is important that you do the emotional work first, making it part of your day, otherwise you simply won't want to eat in the way that you feel you ought.

There are three simple ways to allow your eating habits to lead you to your feelings. You can use this technique every time you are about to eat something:

1. Ask yourself how you are feeling before you eat. Be specific, for example, "I am feeling a bit irritable but quite energetic," and refuse to

*

Food and emotions are strongly linked. The food that you choose to eat and the way you eat it is a reflection of your emotional state. Changing your emotions can bring about a much healthier way of eating.

placate yourself by saying something like "I feel fine really, considering it's the morning."

2. Ask yourself how you expect to feel after you have eaten the thing you are about to eat. Make sure you are specific, for example, "I am hoping to feel more energetic, more cheerful, happier because it tasted great."

3. Ten minutes after you have eaten, ask yourself again how you feel, and be patient enough with yourself to listen to the answer.

If you do this, around mealtimes and snacks over the course of three or four days, you will find out an amazing amount about why you eat, what the food you eat actually does for you, and whether or not you are feeding yourself, or subconsciously doing something else entirely.

Once you know how your emotional life is connected to the way in which you eat, you can take action to find other ways to support yourself in your emotional process. In other words, address the issues that your emotions are flagging up for you instead of trying to alter your feelings by eating.

Food that feeds Water Chi

Now that you are able to take on board and fully accept the role emotion plays in the way in which we feed ourselves, it will be so much more fun to participate in the rest of the five element food journey. Hopefully there is some food in your life that is feeding you right down to your roots—this is the food that makes your body and soul purr with anticipation as you smell it cooking. Water time is wintertime, so you've usually come indoors to eat, unless there is a huge log fire and layers of wraps and hats to huddle under, while the frosty earth cracks under foot. Winter eating should always be incredibly sensuous, appealing to your deepest instincts and senses.

We all know that we should be eating slow-cooked casseroles and quantities of root vegetables, legumes, and preserved local fruits at this time, but what about banning frozen food from the winter kitchen, or only giving space to warmed salads, mildly spiced drinks, and food that glows amber, red, or gold to warm our own slow-burning winter fires?

One of the most powerful things that you can do for your health this winter is to abandon all package opening as from the autumn equinox, and

Ginger has been used in China for thousands of years. Adding it to a meal brings a hint of the exotic and its healing properties aid circulation and help you to beat the wintertime blues.

Winter is a great time to cook. You have the time, you get warm while you do it, you always cook too much for one, so often end up eating in company.

actually cook all the food that you are going to eat. That way you can chose the ingredients, spices, and cooking styles that will actually feed you, rather than just fill you up. Winter is a great time to cook. You have the time, you get warm while you do it, you always cook too much for one, so often end up eating in company. Winter cooking is creative and fills the house with chi, the way turning up the heating and opening the microwave never did!

The aromas that spill from your winter hearth will all warm and stimulate the senses. Add garlic and ginger to every stew, before putting the lid on and letting it alone to cook, slow and generous through the daylight hours. Eat just as dusk first gathers, and settle down to digest the very same chi that you have been cultivating yourself today.

The winter is not the time to be consuming large quantities of ice cold food or fluid. In any case, you will only crave these if you have been spending huge amounts of time shut in overheated spaces, or have become out of rhythm with your natural cycle. Think again as you reach for a cold beer, and choose a beautiful heavy crystal glass with some mulled wine instead. Maybe then you will feel like turning the central heating down a few degrees and breathing a little easier.

It is widely acknowledged by herbalists that adding garlic to slow-cooking casseroles not only adds flavor and depth, but it safeguards you from winter illnesses and its intensity warms you from the inside out.

Winter Food

According to the saying, "that which we hold in our hand we take in to our heart," and when it comes to food, we take it right into our stomachs too! The quality of the whole experience every time we eat is crucial to the quality of chi that the experience engenders.

Especially in wintertime when just about everything you eat is cooked, this process begins with the quality of the hearth that you chose to cook at. The hearth is a place, not a cooking device. It is a center for the wonderful alchemy that happens when food and heat and heart come together.

So make sure yours is a good one. Buy a smaller fridge or freezer, a less expensive, food processor or wok, but make sure that you create a wonderful hearth. Choose a good spot, in a great room, with plenty of light (east- or southeast-facing makes great food). Install the best oven you could ever dream of, add all the other ingredients that will be essential to your style of cooking, arrange all your utensils within one pace distant, add some of your favorite accessories, and the stage will be set. Leave the whole thing to settle down for 24 hours or so, and return, ready to cook!

How about creating a real Water chi-boosting breakfast in bed to celebrate the opening of your hearth? What could be more sensuous than a series of bowls and platters of warmed, aromatic foods eaten back in the many layered and (hopefully) sensuous winter nest? What a great sprawling, messy, flowing, and overflowing feast this will be, and now that your Water energy is balanced, why not revel in it?

You could choose to design a meal that allows all the autumn fruits a place. Cook the fruits, separately, or in combinations to taste, (for example, apples stewed with blackberries and cinnamon, or pears baked with

Breakfast in Bed suggestions?

- compote
- toast
- hot cereal
- herbal tea
- homemade bread
- pancakes
- kedgeree
- muffins
- warm croissant
- French toast
- oatmeal

When the warmth of cooking fills the house, bed is a great place for breakfast—the perfect place to enhance your Water chi.

loganberries and ginger), and serve it all warm, with ground and finely chopped nuts. Once you have begun, let your imagination run wild, cooking all the wonderful foods naturally available during the winter months. Breakfast is an important meal, especially in the winter and deserves your best attention. Why not always aim to eat some warm cooked food soon after rising during this time, and be prepared to eat less heavily in the evening. That way you will rest better, and wake ready to eat.

If you can find people who are happy to join you at breakfast, so much the better, but time alone to reflect while you cook and eat will be a great way to start a day that may not have too much space in it for that unique, and one and only you!

2

Spring/Wood

Introduction

Something rather wonderful and truly magical happens as winter runs its course and moves toward its close. As yin grows into its most extreme manifestation, and energy is laid low and dissipated as far as the eye can see, a universal impulse to maintain life ignites the tiny remnant of yang chi that is held in the midst of overwhelming winter. This spark begins its forward thrust toward the eventual dawning of the new day, the new year, toward spring.

The dawning of spring happens long before most of us see evidence of this new, and often long awaited, beginning. The upturn of chi that makes this new beginning a possibility, is a movement produced by the dynamic between the universal forces of yin and yang, interacting constantly to maintain balance. So, as yin reaches its most extreme moment, yang begins to move into position to bring balance. As yang begins to grow, the whole impetus of chi changes direction, a time, (or a space in time in Feng Shui terms), of great power, vulnerability, instability, and momentum. This transformation is facilitated by the action of the fifth element, Earth, which we will look at later in the book. This moment of changing direction takes us from midwinter toward the beginnings of spring, from midnight toward the first lights of dawn. It takes us from the motionless time of deep reflection, toward the first spark of an idea, when the first movement toward a later action is made.

So, without winter, there could be no spring, and the more completely we have allowed winter to happen, or accepted Water chi, the more space we have created for the first spark of springtime, of Wood energy, to grow. The deeper you go, the higher you can fly, when the time comes!

Let's look a little more closely at the nature of the yang chi that facilitates this upturn. Yang is all about function, direction, purpose, and action. It is the activity, heat, dryness, and propulsion forward that is sustained and balanced by yin's cool receptivity. It is gathered chi, ever moving toward a position of more directed action. It is the dynamic movement to yin's passive moment, the heat of the Sun, to yin's cool of

*

Even during the dead of winter, when all around seems barren, the view of the solitary winter tree is more than a poignant reminder of life—it is the spark of yang in a yin landscape.

the Moon. Without the gathering force of yang chi, springtime wouldn't happen. Without this flame ignited in the midst of the gloom, Water would not transform to Wood.

The quiet contemplation of yin is about to evolve into life-giving yang. Our acceptance of Water will allow the Wood element to flourish—spring will follow winter.

Understanding this action of yang enables us to really appreciate the qualities manifested by the Wood element, which carries within it a sense of purpose and movement toward a goal. This creative impulse of chi, the ideas, plans, and strategies, will all find full expression as actions in the following summer (Fire) phase.

Feng Shui
Spring: Wood Chi explored

Wood, in balance, is a wonderfully creative, expansive energy full of the impetus of the new beginnings that are starting to take shape. This fast-growing energy is held firm and stable by the developed root system at its base, and is protected above ground by its flexibility, its ability to move in the face of change, in the face of the fast-flowing chi of the wind. Often Wood chi is referred to as "tree chi." The Chinese character for Wood depicts a tree, but significantly a large proportion of the character is taken up with the root system, in acknowledgement of the need for stability and nourishment during the process of growth and development.

If Wood is not fed and secure at its base, it can be thrown off balance by the very energy that promotes it. Undernourished Wood, assailed by this great impetus to grow, develop, and change, can lose its grounding, and in a desperate attempt to hold firm, further lose another of its greatest assets, its flexibility. Growing increasingly rigid and brittle in an attempt to regain stability, drawing in tighter, the flow of chi will lose its fluidity and reduce even further its ability to nourish itself.

In human terms this describes a highly motivated individual with great ambition and ability to organize and plan, who attempts to surge forward too fast, perhaps without having spent time reflecting on the appropriateness or scale of his plans at that time, perhaps without fully

Wood, in balance, is a wonderfully creative, expansive energy full of the impetus of the new beginnings that are starting to take shape.

Undernourished Wood can lose its grounding and its flexibility, growing increasingly rigid and brittle in an attempt to regain stability and to nourish itself.

In the same way that strong roots anchor great trees, so our emotional support system enables us to flourish. Without strengthening our roots we too become fragile brittle plants clinging to life's cliff.

acknowledging the importance of allowing his supporting team (his roots), to participate fully in his project. As things begin to go wrong, this type will automatically work harder and faster, tightening the reins of control, pulling back closer to the structures he has put in place. As he gets more frustrated in his attempts to reach his goal in this very single-minded fashion, irritation and anger will set in pulling him further away from the creative thinking and flexibility that initiated the whole project, and on which all earlier success was based. The end point of this process may be the progression of anger and rage into apathy and depression, when increasingly active attempts to correct the situation have all pulled it further off course.

The usual physical manifestations of this process could be any of the following; aches and pains, especially across the shoulders and neck, headaches, even migraines, menstrual disorders and cramps, problems with eyesight, such as blurred vision, and many, many more symptoms all stemming from Wood imbalance. So, Wood chi, like any other, is powerful and creative, when in balance. Out of balance, it is quite a different matter!

Constructing Creative Spaces

Cultivating Wood chi will allow you to be focused in your emotions so that you can plan and face the future with certainty. This can only happen if you are prepared, if your space, and the you it reflects, are ready.

Here is a question designed to find out how the Wood element of the Feng Shui of your space is faring. Is your space structured in a way that makes it easy for you to look ahead, and to make plans that will allow you the full force of your creative expression?

To break the question down:

1.   When you are in your home, is there any place that you can go and look way out into the distance?

2.   Is your home structured in such a way that moving around is simple and straightforward? Or do you have to circumnavigate your way from A to B via lots of places you didn't really want to go, or past lots of things that simply get in your way?

3. Does your space feel like a good place in which to be creative and spontaneous? Is it a place where you can act freely whenever you want to, or are you restricted in your behavior, movement, or self-expression when you are there?

Questions like these can have disconcertingly revealing answers. Maybe you have never considered any of these points when choosing and arranging a space. Maybe you have never viewed the following as priorities, or even as assets:

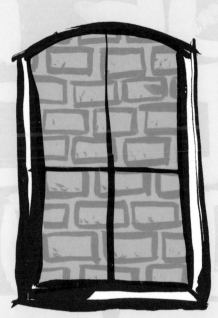

1. Accessibility of long-term views and the ability to look way ahead,

2. The ease with which you can move from one position to another, or

3. The need to have a safe space in which to be creative.

*

Gaining a long-term view can be taken literally— finding a space within your home for wide visions, and making a place to be creative will allow you to make goals and reach destinations.

This may be because you have addressed these needs in other areas of your life. Maybe you go sailing or hiking and have built ease of vision into your life that way. Maybe you have made your work space super-efficient as a space in which to plan ahead, process ideas, and talk strategy, surrounding yourself with people and resources of all kinds to make that process a perfect joy. You may spend so many hours in art therapy, and even more creative pursuits, that all you want to do at home is sleep.

Who knows, but it is my guess that if your home enjoys none of the three elements listed above, it may indicate that your life could be substantially improved by examining at least one of them.

Constructing Creative Spaces 2

A list of practical suggestions can help get you started to balance the Wood chi in your life. All these practical actions will support your own Wood chi. They may not have the results that you expected, but if you take action, things will change for you.

You may wish to clear windows of obstructions either from the inside, or the outside, or in extreme cases, on both. Notice the quality of view that you enjoy from each of your windows. Look especially at the windows at the front of your house, or by your front door. What picture of your future do you see? How could you improve your view? Have the trees you let grow to give you privacy ended up limiting your vision? Consider removing plants and trees that restrict your view at the front of your house, or to the east. If your only long view is in another direction, consider clipping trees or plants that are growing there. If you still have no view, consider importing one in the form of a photograph or painting of a wonderful land- or seascape. You could also try regularly stopping to enjoy the view during the course of your day. Personally I think that a real view is almost essential; art can only add to life, not replace it.

Actively create ease of passage through your space. Attend to gates, drives, paths, doorways, lobbies, halls, and corridors. Clean them, mend them, clear them, up-grade, and positively prioritize them. Put your resources into getting your life moving freely, effortlessly, consistently. Make all slopes in your space an asset—if you have a slope, inside or out, you will know what I mean!

Ask yourself in what ways your space is restricting you. If you want to make more noise, create space where you can be noisy. Be prepared to move things around and put some resources behind your designs. If you feel hemmed in and limited in your ability to do the things that you want to because of lack of space, choose life! Clear some clutter—especially the really big pieces of furniture

The space outside your home invites and welcomes energy into your life. Make sure the entry to your home invites the energy you need.

that only fit in one place or are built-in. Even more importantly, remove anything that makes you feel less than fabulous, even for that moment before your brain told you to be sensible. If they are in your way, move them on. It's your chi or theirs!

Also consider adding opportunities to be more spontaneous or free into your space. Change that solid metal bedstead to a futon that lets you sleep in a different place each night, if that captures your imagination. Or simply install a trampoline in your front garden if that does! The point is, take one good, well-intentioned piece of action to turn your winter into spring, or your headache into a realizable vision of your future.

Clearing out junk within your home does more than move out the old allowing you to move on, it gives you the physical space to make creative, energy-raising places.

Raising the level of Chi

The Feng Shui cures that we have been looking at up to now in this springtime section have all been structural. Wood chi has a lot to do with creating structures (making plans), so that energy can be moved forward toward a recognizable, and realistically attainable goal. But within the structure we need the ability to flow, to be flexible, creative, and spontaneous.

Clearing your living and working areas of accumulated rubbish and clutter in a "Clutter Bust" will, on a practical level, make your home and work-space easier to live in, and on an emotional level it will free your mind from past tensions and frustrations allowing you to concentrate on your present and face the future more positively.

With this in mind, let's move on to boosting the overall levels of chi, and look at some ways to do this that will apply equally well to your living and your working space. These are all incredibly simple, and each decision and action you take will contribute toward your own personal expression of Wood chi.

The most powerful springtime Feng Shui cure is the, by now, well known "Clutter Bust." This is covered in some detail in *Feng Shui In Ten Simple Lessons*, and I will only say that if you just do one thing suggested in this book, then please make it a "Clutter Bust"! Start in whichever part of your space drives you the craziest with its buildup of toxic waste, and systematically and ruthlessly work through your whole space, being particularly ruthless in the darkest cupboards and most inaccessible spaces of your attic.

As you clear your way through your space, notice where the clutter buildup is at its worst, the particular

A Feng Shui "Clutter Bust" is more than a mere tidy-up. Busting clutter is a way to learn about yourself: to examine how you were in your past and how those sides of you which you haven't managed to let go still effect you. The bravest thing you will do is to let go of the mementoes which hold you back. It's a difficult thing to do, but when finished you will be free to face your future more positively.

nature of the items causing the chi traffic jam. Read the message this information is giving you about where you need to allow yourself to let go of the past and move on in your life.

Do you have piles of books and files relating to past success (or even failure)? Move them on and make the space in your life to learn something new. Or maybe you have bought dozens of potions and lotions hoping that they would transform you into a person that someone would really love? Do something right now that will make you love yourself more—a smile

will do for a start. You could try selecting five bottles from your collection—one to enhance each element. This is a great way to focus on the job you want each cosmetic to do for you and a great way to clear the clutter from the rest.

Clearing clutter is the single quickest way to get your chi, and your life, moving. It is the most powerful tool that you have at your disposal, it costs nothing, and even doing the smallest amount will change your life.

Don't forget the "hidden clutter" stored on your computer, in address books, in your paper filing system, and in your outside spaces. As you clear clutter, you will find yourself looking at all the different parts of your life, and having to do some emotional clutter busting too.

Space Clearing

You may need to wash your clothes and hair very frequently during this process, due to all the "psychic junk" flying around. "Psychic junk" is a term coined to describe redundant energy patterns that hang around spaces and people until they are actively moved on. You can move "psychic junk" on by Space Clearing living and working spaces (see *Feng Shui In Ten Simple Lessons* for a complete guide to this wonderful traditional art), or by simply spring-cleaning with the clear intention in your mind "out with the old, in with the new."

Many traditional methods of housekeeping played a great part in keeping the chi in a space sparkling, and springtime is a great time to reestablish some of the most powerful ones:

• The practice of airing things outside to keep them dust- and infection-free is a wonderful way to boost chi.

• Air quilts, pillows, and cushions outside on bright crisp days all through the year (an especially good remedy to help sleep problems and the inability to think clearly).

• Use natural products to clean and polish manually, putting your good clear energy into a space—they will make it sing in a way that nothing else can. This will lift the whole energy of your space.

• Many people now look to the natural aromas of peppermint, basil, and thyme to brighten the chi of their workplaces, while harsh cleaning and disinfecting agents need have no place in a home. Essential oils, used in water (or airborne), are at least as effective and do not pollute the space as they clean, (lavender, citrus, tea tree, and thyme are all good, even in a house where animals and children live alongside one another).

• Change heavy winter curtains, rugs, and colors for light, liberating textures that are less dense and will lift your chi. You can store the cleaned and carefully packed items until the autumn when you will be glad to build those layers back in to your life.

• As you do this, rearrange room layouts, and even locations, to suit the spring upturn of energy.

Clearing Space is more than a good spring-clean—thoroughly clean your rooms, open up and reinvent your space for this new season.

This could mean rearranging your space so that you can sit by a window to eat or work, or moving your office to a room with an easterly or southern aspect. It will mean taking a good look at the space that removing some of your winter furnishings and decorations (and some of the clutter that has built up) has left behind and considering whether the color scheme and overall design still suits you.

Remember you can use these cures any time your Wood chi needs a boost. So if you are sinking too far into a mire of introspection or feel absolutely stuck for ideas or new energy, midsummer or midwinter, these Wood chi cures will work just as well then. Each element has its part to play all through the year, it is simply a shift of emphasis that occurs as the year moves through the seasons, or as a person moves through his/her life.

Washing your hair outside in a spring garden will shake off the winter stillness and invigorate you with Wood chi.

The Garden in Spring

Although outside space in a home is important all year round, it is often the first signs of spring that turn our attention to our garden. Most people now recognize the role the location of their home plays in their life, and have added to that an acknowledgement of the ways in which an interior can support them, but what of the part the land immediately surrounding our space plays?

We are aware that is good to have a house built on a balanced plot, with space distributed to the front and back, and sides where that is possible. We have considered creating support at the back of our house, and openness at the front, and we are aware that the way land slopes, and the location of ponds, trees, and garden structures can have an impact on our chi, and therefore our lives (see *The Feng Shui Directory*). We already know that it is worth spending some time considering the way that our gardens are supporting our ability to grow, develop, and move on in our lives, so let's begin to build on this instinct.

A simple tour of your garden, or what passes for a garden, will tell you a lot about the messages that you are sending to the universe about how you expect your life to be, and what better time than a beautiful spring morning to do just this. Here your ability to organize, plan, and structure will be on full display, either painfully obvious by its absence, or strikingly evident in its complete domination of all spontaneous impulse and the resultant sterility of the space. Tidy but totally uninspiring! You may have become adept at disguising signs and symptoms of Wood imbalance in the

A garden is more than a place in which to relax, it is a reflection of our emotional wellbeing and is both influenced by, and can influence, the way we feel about ourselves.

rest of your life, but the evidence of a garden doesn't lie. Here, as elsewhere, you are aiming for balance, with structure serving as a stage for spontaneity and natural expression.

If your outside space has become something close to an outside storage area for junk, with neglected plants, paths, and scrub grass vying for space with disused household paraphernalia, you will need to do as much clutter clearing here as you can bear before the natural design of the space will begin to emerge.

If you (or a previous owner) have imposed an idea of how it should be on your garden that has little to do with its intrinsic nature and lots to do with practicality and fashionable aesthetics, you may need to unravel a considerable amount of this imposed structure. Remove anything from trees to fences or misplaced ponds, then you can add elements that will allow the natural expression of the space its true voice.

You will come to understand the way the garden needs to be by spending time out in it, rather than by being indoors looking out. Gardening books will tell you all you need to know about caring for your space at this time of year. By bringing your understanding of the nature of Wood chi into that work, you will be opening your garden and your life up to a completely new dimension!

Your garden should be able to express its own nature and your emotional balance.

A simple tour of your garden will tell you a lot about the messages that you are sending to the universe about how you expect your life to be, and what better time than a beautiful spring morning to do just this.

Emotional Wellbeing
Introduction

Springtime is the time to come out of our shells, to grow, to change, to get active, to reach for the sky, and make plans for how we are going to get there. Time to shake ourselves awake and alive, get moving, have a good look at what's out in the big wide world, and figure out the part we can play in it. Scary or inspiring?

A large part of your response will depend on your attitude to change, because the ability to accept change and embrace it, as part of a developing life, is integral to your ability to weather spring and the huge amount of change it brings with it. Some people consider themselves to be able to adapt to change really well, even to welcome change, or go looking for it. But what about the type of change that isn't within your control—maybe by its very nature is beyond your control—that arrives to crash all your own plans and expectations and replace them with something completely unexpected, something that you may have even wished to avoid at all costs?

Our ability to accept change and turn it to good use, whatever its nature, depends largely, in my experience, on our ability to trust. If we can trust that we will be able to learn from our changing circumstances, adapt, and quickly move into a position of balance in our new situations, then we will be accepting of, and will survive in good form, all sorts of circumstances. However, for some people an apparently small change to one of their "structures" will throw them completely off balance and into a state of dysfunctioning disarray, that takes them further and further away from a position of strength.

Springtime is the time for change and development.

> The ability to accept change and embrace it, as part of a developing life, is integral to your ability to weather spring and the huge amount of change it brings with it.

For others, the large degree of inner strength and integrity that their emotional life gives them allows them to flourish under what, for some others, would be an alarming amount of disruption, which would bring them to a state of collapse. So how do you move into a position where change, of any kind, becomes a source of strength?

This is where our understanding of the interconnectedness of the five elements begins to be a huge asset. If you were able to read and experience the first section on Water chi, you will by now appreciate the value of supporting your store of inner strength and some of the ways you can do that. Experiencing the ability to trust and feel safe—one of the results of this awareness—is crucial to your ability to be able to develop by accepting and using change.

If you cannot risk experiencing change, then you must stay as you are, which is to turn your back on the very core experience of being alive. Many of us expend huge amounts of energy attempting to control our lives. Ironically, we very often do this by looking forward and planning new developments for ourselves, but with a rigidity that eliminates all real possibility for growth. This is a way of being that has little to do with being at ease with the business of being alive and trusting in the process, and much to do with trying to reduce anxiety.

Emotional Life

If, for example, you trust yourself to be able to adapt to any situation and get the best out of it, you needn't fear change, and the enormous potential for growth and development it brings with it. If you have put a structure into position, expecting it to help you to attain one of your goals, (this may be very simple—something like a plan for going out for the evening), and something comes along to threaten or change it, a common response would be disappointment, often disguised as irritation. Depending on the scale or frequency of your frustration, you may respond with increasing anger, or, in the long term, rage. If your Wood energy is very out of balance, it may not take much to destabilize you, and sometimes the irritability, or repressed anger, can become endemic throughout your whole life.

If, however, you can cultivate a flexibility born out of your trust in your ability to make a success of any situation (not to be thrown off balance by events around you), then you can move into a position where you can actually strengthen your Wood chi, and reduce the associated emotional and physical symptoms that come when it is out of balance.

Anger has a valuable role to play as part of our defense mechanism, part of our survival tool kit, but so often in current living, we fail to identify actions that we could be making to change our lives for the better, by simply responding over and over again to situations with irritation or anger. The caricature of an uptight, stressed-out person, who bristles with righteous indignation at all the wrongs that have been done to them by people getting in the way of their ability to control their surroundings, is all too familiar. An exaggerated single-mindedness, an obsession with seeing a particular task through to completion is often part of the picture. This kind of rigidity of thought and action, is often just the flip side of a wonderful ability to innovate, plan, and organize; it is Wood out of balance.

If you recognize yourself in this picture, you may wish to follow these suggestions for action. They will help to return you to your wonderful creative, easy self.

> If you can cultivate a flexibility in your trust in your ability to make a success of any situation, you can actually strengthen your Wood chi.

- Fall in with someone else's plans for the day, and follow their lead.
- Ask yourself when you last did something really spontaneous, or broke your own rules.
- Sit down and list your main objectives in life. Is your current action bringing you closer toward them, or have you lost sight of where you are actually going?
- Spend more time every day listening to other people and watching the way that they approach life.

Next time something goes wrong, take a deep breath, let it go, smile, and see it as a chance to do something differently.

Being adaptable to change will make the flow of your life run more smoothly. Recognize the emotions which hinder this, and your journey will be made easier.

Wood energy

The great innovators, inventors, and revolutionaries of our time are all spurred on by Wood. They can all stand alone, single-minded in their ambition to bring to fruition something they know to be of great future potential. But they all need Fire as much as they needed Water to create the source of their power and flexibility. It is the alchemy of yang bursting out of yin and moving to its extreme as Fire that is the essence of life.

So, as yang energy grows at springtime, it must keep within it the flexible, malleable, receptive quality of Water, of yin, if it is to endure. Fire, the fruition of growth, is the direction toward which Wood is moving, but Water is still the source. If Wood is out of balance then, there are two ways to remedy it. Firstly, to support it at its base, by attending to Water. Secondly, to give it room for expression, somewhere to express its excess, by paying attention to Fire.

For your plans and dreams to be realized you need to balance Wood chi with each of the other four elements.

Someone who has become very high-minded, self-opinionated, and generally uptight could do no better than seek the following cures:

o Laughter: if you have a headache, go and see a comedy.

o Action: if your muscles ache with tension, go and have a swim.

o Passion: don't be irritable, be passionate!

There are times when laughter, action, or passion seem a million miles away, and these are often the times when we need them most. If these times close in on you, my best advice would be to be a little less tough on

Lessons of joy can be learned from daffodils—they, rest in winter, bud and flower in spring.

yourself. Repeat to yourself; I have the potential to laugh, act, and be passionate, if I take a little time out from my current (self-imposed?) schedule, they will all come back and find me where we left off.

Be generous with yourself as never before. Lose the pressure and boring repetition from your life, and all will be well.

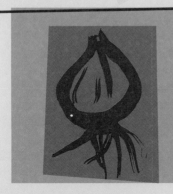

Yoga
Forward bend from squat

This asana is designed to increase flexibility and calm the mind, so that thinking can become clearer and life can flow a little more easily. Enjoy the sensation of your body opening, being present for every moment of the journey this asana takes you on. There is no end goal.

1. start from a squatting position on the floor with your feet parallel and hip width apart, your hands firmly against the ground and your head dropped.

2. take some time to release your neck fully and let the weight of your head help your spine to release. Remember to allow your face to relax! You may feel tightness in the part of your body that carries most tension.

3. use complete breaths to help release that tension through a loose mouth, allowing your abdomen to expand as you inhale.

4. spend some time in this position, feeling your back, neck, and shoulders releasing and a sense of calm filling your mind.

The weight of your head will help you to unravel if you let it. Don't worry if your legs aren't straight, keep your contact with the ground through your hands and feet, and your breath will do the rest.

When you are ready, you may wish to continue into the next stage. Let your head remain heavy and dropped downward, keeping a strong awareness of your feet and hands against the ground and, with your next slow exhalation, move your heels to contact the ground, and lift your hips toward the sky.

When you can go no further without losing contact between your hands and the floor, stay for a few breaths before returning to your original position. Without any sensation of hurrying toward an end position, repeat the movement three more times, each time paying as much attention to your head, feet, hands, and breath. After some time of practicing this movement, you may end up with your legs straight and the palms of your hands resting on the ground. If you do, enjoy the sensation of one continuous movement from the ground, through your feet, growing up through your legs and releasing through freely moving hips and down through the whole length of your spine and into the ground through the palms of your hands.

This asana is extremely good for balancing your Wood chi and is worth persevering with, although the backs of your legs may complain. Don't worry about the sensation of stretching through your legs, as long as you are not forcing your body and trying to achieve some self-imposed goal, all will be well.

Make a friend of your breath as it guides your body to open where it needs to most, and be aware of the way in which you are contacting the ground throughout.

The affirmation for this asana is "I am happy to change."

A variation of Tree Asana

Having brought the feet into contact with the ground in the last asana, we will develop this feeling in the following pose, which involves making a good connection with the ground, and then growing out of this to stretch up toward the sky. This is a pose about rising Wood chi, and the need to establish our roots and grounding in order to remain in balance and stable as we grow ever upward.

Allow all responsibility to slide from your shoulders as your energy drops down through your roots, and pulses up through your center.

1.   spend some time standing on two legs to begin with every time you practice this asana.

2.   stand with your feet parallel and hip width apart. Imagine that the soles of your feet are the palms of your hands and become acutely aware of every sensation that they are reporting back to you.

3.   with each exhalation, extend your awareness right down through your body, legs, and feet and down into the floor. Feel as though you are rooted into the floor. This will help in all your standing poses, especially the ones where you may find balancing hard.

4.   when you are ready extend one arm skyward, keeping both your shoulders relaxed downward. You may begin with fingers pointed up, but eventually aim to flex your hand at the wrist and open the palm of your hand toward the sky. This opening of hands and feet is a very important part of all yoga, so try and include it from early on in your practice.

5.   as you stand like this, feel the balance of your body undisturbed, your shoulders and hips still aligned with each other, your neck long, and your breath unrestricted.

The affirmation for this asana is "Flexibility is my strength."

Once you are very at home with this movement, (try with the left and right arms extended one after the other), you may wish to move on.

As you exhale, and while your arm is extended, shift your weight slightly so that you can release one foot from the floor, bending your knee, and catching your foot in your hand behind your hip. Keep your knees aligned and your supporting leg strong. Aim to feel as though you are lifting out of your hips, with your torso and arm rising upward.

Concentrate on the rising chi as you inhale, and a dropping back down through the back of your body, through your ankle and foot into the ground, as you exhale.

The more you stretch up and concentrate on keeping your supporting leg strong, the more you can enjoy the sensation of growing and being in balance all at the same time. The important thing is to keep your breath flowing, and to keep the asana alive. Don't worry about swaying or moving a little, flexibility will keep you upright!

*

Watch out for your ribs moving too far forward as you extend into this stretch, and let your hips drop steadily downward.

A series of movements for shoulders, arms, and upper back

Leave your body still and centered as your shoulders move with the freedom of release.

I always like to do these asanas in a series as I love the feeling of energy flowing back into my body as I release tension and flush out toxins. Do these asanas standing, feet parallel and hip width apart, preparing as in the previous asana.

First interlace your fingers and enjoy stretching your whole hand as you turn your palms away and extend your arms in front of you. Pause for a few breaths before allowing your hands to travel in a wide arc in front of you, until you can take them no further without disturbing the position of your torso. Avoid sticking your ribs forward, lifting your shoulders toward your ears, bending your arms at the elbows, or stopping with your palms facing directly upward toward the sky. Stay in your final position for some breaths allowing your shoulders and shoulder blades to drop downward and your upper arms to release.

Meanwhile, check that the tension from your upper body hasn't found a new home somewhere else. Now do this in reverse.

Start by rolling your shoulders up and back, linking your hands behind your back, with both arms straight. Avoid pushing your chest forward at this point and concentrate on your inhalation.

Slowly lift your hands, feeling your upper back and arms slowly stretching. You may wish to allow your head to drop gently back. Allow your body to hold the position and take a few deep inhalations in this position to complete the asana.

For this next posture you can either kneel on the floor with your feet tucked under your hips, or sit in virasana (hero's pose), with your legs to either side of your hips and the tops of your feet against the floor.

The affirmation for this asana is 'I am free to breathe effortlessly and completely'.

Be careful not to stress or twist your knees—you may want to place some cushions under your hips in order to be able to settle down against the ground. For this asana it is a good idea to carefully study the illustration before beginning:

1. begin by lifting one arm straight up, bending it at the elbow, and dropping it down to catch the other hand.

2. if you can't reach your lower hand, extend your stretch by using a sock, scarf, or tie to bridge the space between the two hands. One side will be easier than the other!

3. again avoid sticking your ribs out as you do this asana and be aware of the position of your spine. You should have a sensation of lifting up away from your hips, with the curve of your neck remaining soft throughout.

Trikonasana

This asana is particularly beautiful and in itself becomes an affirmation of opening up to the opportunities that life has to offer us. I teach it as the enacting of a greeting to each new day. Try practicing the asana if you are feeling anxious or in low spirits. If you are conscientious about holding the position for at least a minute, (considerably more if it is comfortable and you can keep the asana alive), your emotional state will follow the example of your body and begin to feel stronger and more confident.

> The affirmation for this asana is "Every day I begin a new journey."

The wide base held throughout this asana makes a statement about your ability to be expansive and powerful, while the arm and head lifting to the sky is unconditionally positive and forward-looking. Your perspective on life will be turned around while the wide open arms and chest and back make for free breathing and gently open your heart.

When practicing this asana, as with any other, treat your movement into, and out of, it as important parts of the journey.

*

Pay careful attention to the shape you make with your feet, lining up your front heel with the instep of the back foot.

1. begin with your legs about a step and a half apart, with your feet parallel.

2. be careful that as you turn one foot out you don't follow it with your torso; the leg revolves in the hip, while everything else stays looking forward.

3. lift your arms as though they were wings and you were about to take flight, allowing energy to flow from the center of your body at the front and the back to feed them, and allow the palms of your hands to open so that your finger can uncurl and come alive. Treat yourself to a smile!

4. the next movement is best described as the action of reaching for something just beyond your grasp, something that is at shoulder height. Don't collapse through your legs as you do this; maintain your strong lively base.

Your legs will feel strong and alive so that your upper body can move freely at your hips.

5. allow the outreaching hand to float down to meet your leg, while the other arm and hand lift, as in making a motion of waving or greeting. Use the strength of your torso and legs to support yourself and avoid leaning on your bottom hand!

At first, practice with your face looking forward into the day, but in time you may wish to turn your head to look first at your uplifted shoulder and then continue your gaze up toward the sky and beyond.

Be very present throughout your body as you maintain this asana, allowing your inhalation to energize you and your exhalation to calm and ground you. In time this way of practicing will become a meditation in itself. You should feel the front and the back of your body opening along one plane, as though you were flying. Practicing this posture will strengthen your legs, stomach, and back. Your shoulders should be relaxed throughout.

Repeat the asana for the other side of your body, being aware of this completely different journey.

Trikonasana Variation

This asana will allow you to enjoy stretching your body and opening your mind in a different and slightly more subtle way than the previous asanas. It is best practiced after Trikonasana, because although some people find this easier and less intimidating, to enjoy its full power it is best to have performed the more dramatic version first.

1. create the base of the posture first, measuring one and a half steps between your feet, keeping your feet facing forward. This distance will give you a wide but stable stance.

2. turn one leg out from the hip; one foot will be placed on the floor roughly at right angles to the other. Settle into this new position with your hips both facing forward, legs strong but not braced at the knees, and your feet positioned on the floor so that the toes are spread out and your weight is well balanced between both feet, and between the four corners of each foot.

The affirmation for this asana is "I move with the flow."

Notice how the four corners of each foot stay in contact with the ground throughout, and the way in which your attention to your feet and your ankles allows you to feel secure and strong in these standing poses. As we progress through the Yoga sections of the book, the aim is to build up a range of movements and ways of using the body that eventually become instinctive and are carried through to the rest of our lives. Developing an awareness of the feet is a key to developing an awareness of the way our whole body moves. The aim of all yoga practice is to increase the suppleness, strength, and overall health of our feet, so that they can do the job they were intended to do for the rest of the body. So, in this standing asana, we have time to consider the effect the feet have on the rest of the body.

To begin moving into the asana:

1. spread the feet against the ground and lift up through the ankles. Feel the energy flowing up through your legs, concentrating on this movement as you inhale. Be aware of your hips feeling open and fluid, as your spine lifts you upward.

Allow your waist to lengthen and open as the whole line between your fingertips down to your back foot warms into life.

2. as the rising chi lifts through your body and reaches your heart line, allow your arms to extend out to the sides, opening the palms of your hands and uncurling your fingers, which should begin to tingle with life.

3. from this point lift one arm directly up above your head, letting the other arm drop to your leg. Your arm will describe an arc, which you can follow through until eventually your arm rests horizontal to the ground.

Your hips stay centrally aligned throughout, and the whole of the side of your body enjoys a wonderful stretch.

Halasana the plow

*

Respect this asana and it will provide you with many wonderful gifts.

This asana can be done either with the support of a bed or chair, or just on the ground. It encourages flexibility, locates tension lurking in the upper back and melts it, and gives you a wonderful chi boost.

Always start this asana in a supported way, and remember forcing will not help the parts you want to open, but may strain your neck. Start by lying comfortably on your back with your knees drawn into your chest. Give yourself a good relaxing massage by breathing deeply in this position, and rolling from side to side and backward and forward. Once you are thoroughly warm and relaxed begin to experiment with the feeling of your legs going over your head, still curled up. Using your hands to support your back at this point is a good idea. Once you feel confident that you know what your range of movement is and how it feels to curl up in this way, play with the posture a little, extending one leg, then the other, always moving slowly and within the limits of your own flexibility.

You may wish to spend some days at this level. It is much more important to introduce your body and mind to this asana at a consistent gentle pace with a smile on your face, rather than by gritting your teeth, struggling to breathe, and fighting your way to another version of your old inflexible self! So, keep supple in your attitude, and when your body is ready, find yourself in the supported version of this asana. Keep your back relaxed and don't compromise your breath in order to stay in an uncomfortable position.

When you are ready to move into the full Halasana, allow yourself to feel as though you are unraveling away from your shoulders, spiraling up and over, to fall toward the ground with your legs extended and your feet, as ever, open. In this posture, your shoulders, neck, and head form a steady base, chi is rising up through them and warming the length of your spine.

Allow your neck to feel open and breathe easy as your back opens and your energy unfurls.

As you exhale consciously allow any tension or staleness in your body or mind to fall away through your legs and feet. It will begin to feel as though a wonderful circular movement of chi is flowing through you, revitalizing you as you create more and more space for new life.

Some people find breathing uncomfortable in this asana at first. As you continue to practice it and become fluid, breathing in this position will begin to flow effortlessly.

I have included this, and the previous two asanas, in this section because they introduce such a wonderful new perspective on life, and build confidence and variety into what may have become fairly rigid, monotonous thought patterns and lifestyles.

Food
Food to balance Wood chi

Fruit and vegetables not only taste better the fresher they are, they're better for us too.

It matters to all of us where and how our food is grown. The integrity of the whole growing process, from the source of the seed, or livestock, right through the way in which it was nourished as it grew, to the manner in which it was harvested or slaughtered and brought into the food supply, is important to all of us. To some of us it matters, with fruit and vegetables at least, that they were grown in the same hemisphere, so that we can eat food that our body needs in any one season. We accept the fact that the nutrients our body needs at any one time will be found in food grown relatively locally and relatively recently. We know that frozen or even canned food doesn't quite do it for us—we are lucky to enough to be able to eat really good quality lively food, and we feel different as a result.

If you accept that there is a vast difference in eating between, for example, a home-grown potato pulled fresh from the soil and a similar item bought form a local store, then where does that difference lie? For me it lies in the energetic quality of the potato, in its chi. Eating is a coming together of the chi of the entire life cycle of our food, with our own chi at the moment at which the food is consumed. Our chi at that moment will depend on a whole series of factors: how tired we are, how relaxed, what else we are eating or drinking, who we are with, and so on. The whole of the food's journey to our plate determines the quality of its chi. It is this journey that creates the quality of chi that we absorb when we eat. The nature of these two energies coming together determines the quality of nourishment that the process of eating affords us.

This consideration for the energetic quality of food is fundamental to my approach to eating and nourishing myself, my family, and my friends. It forms the cornerstone for the way in which many people approach eating, but it is something that has been all but lost for many of us—all, but not completely.

* *The journey food takes to reach us is as important as the way it is cooked. The growing, tending and harvesting can add strength to the food which, through eating, is passed on to us.*

Who Cooked Your Dinner Today?

Suggestions

- Try new ways of cooking
- Liven up the kitchen before you begin
- Remove time pressure
- Ask someone else to cook if you are too tired.

We still harbor the last vestiges of an awareness of the energetics of food in the tradition of our eating. Everyone acknowledges for example, that there is nothing quite like their mom's apple pie or roast chicken, or will travel miles to a certain restaurant for the experience of eating pizza there. The cappuccino at one café never tastes anything like the one at another; the way one person mixes a drink cannot be duplicated by someone else however many instructions they take.

I was surprised at the way in which my sons reacted when they both developed a headache immediately after eating dinner the other day. After considering the ingredients of the meal for a moment, and presumably eliminating this as a possible cause, they turned to me and asked me whether I had been particularly stressed while cooking the meal, to which I had to say "yes." I had come home late, I was tired, and some part of me resented having to cook. The boys had assumed a connection between the content of the food we had just eaten, the resultant feeling induced in those eating it, and the chi of the cook, on this occasion, me. I have to say I was immediately aware that I had been pretty irresponsible to cook while in that state of mind.

The Chinese say never eat food in a restaurant when the chef is angry, and throughout Asia there is still an acceptance of the fact that we cook something of ourselves into our food. Meanwhile in the U.K. many women receiving treatment for cancer have reported a change in the quality of their baking. I suggest that we all become more aware of the whole chi picture of the food that we are eating—it will do wonders for our health.

We can all foster certain practices in the kitchen and boost our chi:

• Spend time, even a few moments, creating a happy atmosphere in which to cook. This may mean clearing a good space and gathering all the utensils and ingredients before you begin, or it may mean putting on some music and opening the window. Actively do something that will make the space feel great while you cook.

• Remove time pressure from the list of ingredients for your meal. You may have to delay serving the meal, provide a stopgap snack, or simply serve something fresher and simpler, but don't allow yourself to cook while harassed.

• Know that there are some times when you simply shouldn't be cooking at all. Ask someone else to cook. You might be amazed at the magic that pours out of your kitchen at such times, and the variety that sharing the cooking engenders.

There is no such thing as a person who cannot come up with a plate of something that is good to eat, providing we are prepared to try out some new or oddly novel dishes! The idea of eating food that has been cooked with love, inspiration, or creativity is in itself enough to lift the spirits.

To really nourish our Wood chi we need to eradicate monotony and resentment from our food as much as from any other part of our lives. It is very difficult to feel full of enthusiasm for the newness and interest of life unless our food and its eating reflects just that.

The act of cooking, just as much as the meals prepared, is a way of making you feel good. Both the cook and the eater benefit from the joy of feeding others, and being fed with love.

Eat lively food

Spring is a time for new beginnings. It is a time when everyone's spirits are lifted and energy levels are rising. It makes sense then that it is a time when we can nourish that sense of freshness with the food that we are eating and also, that we are not eating.

Let water revive your Wood chi.

I am not a great believer in diets based on what we should not be eating, and prefer instead to amass great quantities of the food that we absolutely love to eat. It suits my approach to life better. With this in mind, I suggest that springtime is a good moment to go out and get yourself a really good supply of drinking water, the sort you will be actually inspired to drink. Of course having glasses that you just want to get out and use always helps.

Springtime is a good moment to go out and get yourself a really good supply of drinking water, the sort you will be actually inspired to drink.

So put your wine glasses well out of reach and bring down your finest tumblers, because springtime is the occasion on which to crack open the elixir of life itself, and drink water, morning, noon, and night.

Feed your Wood energy, but don't flood it. Remember different people, with different diets need to drink different amounts. As a rule vegetarians will need to drink less than meateaters, and the more active you are the more you will need to drink. If you provide yourself with a supply of delicious water, at a temperature that you like to drink it, you will find that you will drink enough to support your body's needs.

While you are shopping for water, you might look out for all the other fresh lively food that will invigorate your body and clear your mind. Include plenty of fresh growing herbs which you can eat in great handfuls. Their aromas will knock you out with delight, and the texture and taste will wake

*

*Wake up your body as
well as your spirit after
the winter lull with fresh
lively food.*

up your whole being.
Try putting quantities of
whole cilantro in a sandwich
(leaves and stems) with your
favorite filling, or eat a handful of
parsley as you pass through the kitchen.
If you eat it after every meal as well, not only will
your digestion and breath benefit, your teeth will too,
since it is full of iron and calcium. Plant parsley where it
grows best, under rose bushes, and later in the year you can also
eat the rose petals that fall among its branches.

Baby spinach eaten raw with a squeeze of fresh lemon and shavings of
parmesan tossed on top is another treat, to be eaten out of a huge wide
bowl while sitting under a tree in its first leaf. This kind of eating will revive
your Wood chi and bring out the spring in you!

Eating differently to balance Wood

If you think about nourishing yourself energetically by eating, you will be careful, not only about the quality of the ingredients of the food and drink that you give to yourself, or what energy has been added to those ingredients that has altered them, but also the way in which you receive the whole package into your body and how you assimilate and use it.

Once you have started to look at the process of eating in this way you can soon see that eating when really tired or stressed could be quite an odd thing to do to your body. Are you really giving to your body what it wants at any one time?

Maybe it would be better to take a nap before eating that meal, or eat very lightly, even if you had planned to eat a large meal. It would certainly be better to make sure that you don't eat when in the middle of an argument, or when you feel uncomfortable physically or emotionally.

We all know that feeding a small baby when it is distressed is a recipe for disaster, so why do it to yourself?

Your thoughts and feelings, as well as the ability of your body to be in the right state to assimilate the food that you are giving it, are an important part of the process of eating. Eating while neglecting your own state is, I believe, one of the causes of obesity. Once you begin to acknowledge that there is a dynamic between the food you eat and what use your body can, or cannot, make of it, you can start to get the fit between what and when you eat and what and when your body wants you to eat right.

Be conscious of how you feel when you eat, rather than just eating for its own sake.

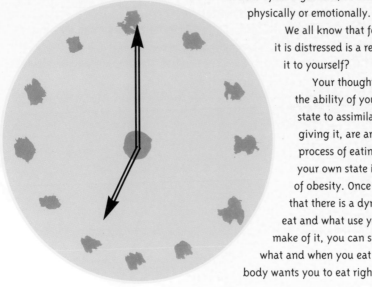

One of the ways to avoid semiconscious habitual eating that may be allowing you to eat without actually feeding yourself appropriately, is to introduce new ways of eating. This may mean eating foods that you haven't eaten before, or cooking foods in different ways, or simply serving them on different crockery, or choosing to eat in a different part of the kitchen or house.

You can at least begin to broaden the range of smells, textures, and tastes that you are presenting to your body. This introduction of newness to your diet will help to increase your awareness of the "when" and "how" of eating, and balance your current emphasis on the "what." You can therefore reduce the stress on your system that comes from introducing unwanted ingredients into it. More of what you eat will be utilized, and less laid waste and stored up as toxic waste, or as fat.

By eating in this way, you will be giving your whole system a real spring treat, and, you will hopefully heighten your awareness of the part that you, as the person actually eating the food, play in your own nutrition.

You can learn to eat the right kind of foods and amounts for you by listening to your body — it knows what's best for it—and then when you've got your food right your body will feel great.

3

Summer/Fire

Summer/Fire chi
Introduction

Fire chi is action unleashed, power made manifest. From the deep pool of contemplation that is Water and wintertime, the germ of an idea condenses. Day dawns from the midst of night, and spring is born out of winter. As spring dawns and Wood chi moves upward, driven by the winds of change, the first thoughts and plans lift to the surface. This gathering chi moves closer, bunching, becoming more and more focused, and is propelled ever higher, as yang builds to its zenith and, with it, summer's height is released from the tight bud of spring. Wood has reached its moment of fullness and can no longer contain its promise and potential. Fire is ignited; from a tight bud a flower head is unfurled and the full splendor of life is there for all to see. This is the time when the promise of spring becomes the reality of summer, the gathering chi of Wood becomes the blazing heat of Fire.

The Fire element is on stage throughout the elemental cycle of the year, dressed in the gaudiest of colors, never too far away from the front of our minds before bursting into life as an expression of what, for many of us, the rest of the process is really all about. It is the action, the party happening, the big performance, the exam eventually sat, the plant blossoming, the deep thinker giving voice. Exposed for all to see, it will be adored if it lives up to expectations, or denounced if it fails to deliver. If Water has been allowed the space and safety to lie low and pool, if spring has risen bright, clear, and flexible, then the fulfillment of summer will be all we wished for, and the performance of a lifetime will be given and enjoyed by all!

> Fire is ignited; from a tight bud a flower head is unfurled and the full splendor of life is there for all to see.

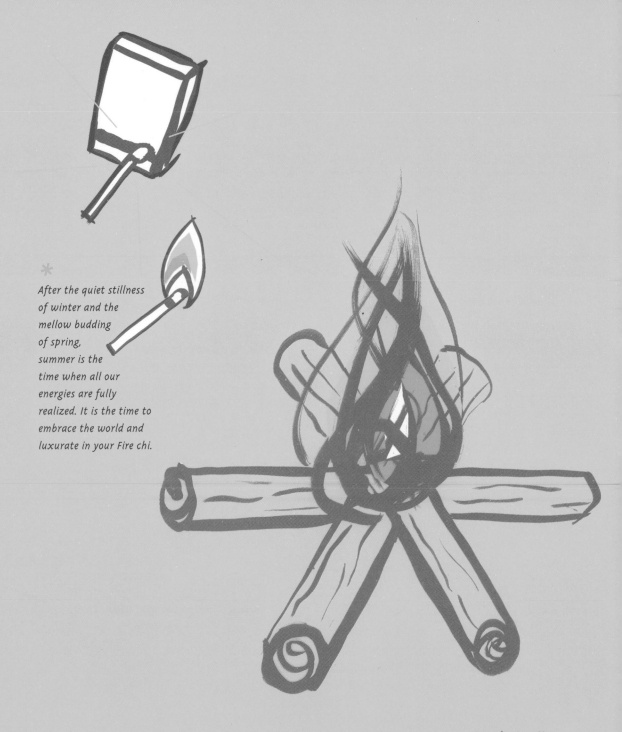

After the quiet stillness of winter and the mellow budding of spring, summer is the time when all our energies are fully realized. It is the time to embrace the world and luxurate in your Fire chi.

During summer, when the Fire element is at its height, it is our hearts that we must listen to and nurture. Taking care of our bodies in this way will enable our emotions to soar and passion to flourish.

The belief that the emotions are not solely governed by, or held, in the brain is part of the Asian world view. Our personality and our approach to life is not only the product of the way our whole being is related to the universe but also the way in which we acknowledge our connection to the chi of all other beings and processes. Within the human body, each set of organs functions to maintain part of the whole body/mind/spirit picture that constitutes the sense of self.

Central to the perception of the role of the element Fire (and all its corresponding processes, such as midday, midsummer, the direction south), is an understanding of the role of the heart, which moves way beyond an appreciation of its purely physiological role and the part it plays in the circulatory system. This is expressed through language when, for example, someone is described as "heartless," or is advised to "have a heart" in order to rescue a situation from a purely logical or cerebral response. We talk about being "big-hearted" (or conversely having "lost heart" in something), to express a sense of being alive, intelligent, and truly human, in a way that moves beyond the limits of logic and thought. Access to this sense of common humanity endows us with an innate morality and connection to something bigger than our individual sense of ourselves.

In Chinese Taoist philosophy, the level of chi that resides in the heart is called Shen. An

> Shen is the spiritual component of chi, the spark of something sacred within each of us. Shen is the recognition that everything in the universe is one.

Shen is at the heart of all things, all that exists within the universe, and at the very heart of the universe itself.

understanding of the role of Shen is central to comprehending the element Fire, the part of the elemental cycle that is expressed as summer, and the concept of the role of the heart. Shen is the spiritual component of chi, the spark of something sacred within each of us. Shen is the recognition that everything in the universe is one, that all duality is illusion, that there is no separation into "us" and "them" (for we are all one), good and bad, (for there is only what "is"), and that within each moment is held the kernel of its opposite, (within yang is the seed of yin, within yin, the spark of yang). Only by cultivating Shen will the Fire element be balanced, helping us to achieve fulfillment.

The concept of Shen in Feng Shui

Cultivating Shen can bring spirituality into your life, and enhance the joy of living and bringing you love, fun, and friends.

Shen is the level of chi that oversees the emotions; it is what we might call "spirit," and as such forms the highest and most refined level of energetics in the universe. So how can Shen be balanced through the practice of Feng Shui? How can something so seemingly ethereal be influenced by the physical details of setting out our living or working space?

Every physical action that you take is both a reflection of yourself, and an affirmation of the energetic space that you are moving toward, (which you create for yourself through thoughts, words, and actions). By changing what you are doing, how you are living, and the space you are living in, you can not only transform your spiritual condition, but also continue to build on that change.

For many of us, awareness of any spiritual connection or condition has become hazy, distant, or even totally unrecognizable, the result of the ways in which the concept of "spirituality" has become packaged or represented. But if we think of spirituality in terms of "heart," a way of operating that extends beyond thought, or even emotion, then it becomes more accessible, and most people immediately recognize it as something that does in fact play a role in their life. Think about the "vague sense" we have about things, the intuitions, the feeling of being "driven" to do something, the "gut feelings." All of these can be built on, and we will feel more warm hearted, brave hearted, and absolutely light hearted as a result!

As you begin to cultivate Fire chi you will find that you are bringing more fun, more laughs, more action, more friends, more communication, more high spirits, good spirits, (more spirit in general) into your life. Plans will be fulfilled and dreams will come true; in other words, summer will come to your garden, your home, and your workplace.

Begin to cultivate the spirit, or Shen, in your life by taking a brief walk to the place from which any passerby would view your house. Look at your

space with an attitude free from judgement, blame, or the division into right and wrong. Nourish your own spirit by approaching this process with compassion, kindness, and generosity.

Take a notebook with you and write down three statements about the message that your space gives to a passerby, based purely on immediate observation of the exterior.

Action to cultivate Shen

Now it is time to give your findings some due consideration, and think about what action you are going to take. Notice that I use the word "action," not plans for the future, ideas to consider, excuses, or justifications for things that you have judged as wrong. Fire is about action, living in the present, so let's see how being active, immediately active, feels.

Review your list of three observations and ask yourself:
- What do they say about the welcome you would provide to a passerby?
- What do they say about your generosity, tolerance, and acceptance?
- What do they say about your ability to be with people, share good times and bad?

If they say very little, then that in itself is worth noticing.

View your home in a positive light and give yourself credit for the positive things you have done for yourself. By accepting what you have achieved you will learn to make your environment ever more nurturing.

Look for anything positive in your findings. Positive observations might include: a wide open driveway or well-lit gateway; abundant vegetation, planted to nurture surrounding wildlife; a swinging seat for two or more people; a cat sitting on a windowsill; signs of life and welcome glimpsed through windows; something humorous by the front door! Look for anything that would make a stranger feel comfortable as they walked up the path and knocked on the door.

Now is the time to add to the positive. You could position something on a windowsill that says "good times" to you, or you could add a bird feeder to a beautiful tree or bush that you already have by your front

gate. To boost a sense of generosity in your space, bring more flowers to sit alongside the ones that are already by your front door.

There is a wonderful house near where I live which is used as a venue for music exams. Whenever I go there, taking one or other nervous examinee, I am impressed by the, I am quite sure, subconscious Feng Shui that has gone on there to improve everyone's performance and lighten their spirits. It is a small terraced house, inauspiciously placed at the end of a road, but what lifts its chi is the fact that the owners have placed a collection of decorative butterflies above the front door, which, on exam days is always left ajar to reveal other light-hearted details along the hallway.

Remember, it is your house to do with what you will, there are no rules; do whatever captures your fancy and makes you smile. Forget the sober, bland house or office next door, and concentrate on attracting lightness of spirit and warm heartedness into your own space.

More action to cultivate Shen

Once you have assessed the exterior of your space, you will find it easier to start making more changes by spending time building on the positive elements. This process will help you to let go of features that you realize you just don't need any more. If, on the other hand, the exterior of your space proclaimed uncompromisingly negative messages, such as "Go away, I'm mean and grumpy" or "Don't look at me, I don't deserve a piece of the action," you will find that it is best to clear these away first, before you start to help your space reveal its more positive side.

Once you have built on the positive elements of the exterior of your space, and wondered to yourself just why you thought a gate that is almost impossible to open and a huge thorny hedge running the length of the driveway were such a good idea in the first place, you may be ready to step inside and have some fun. After all that immediate action, you will be looking for a place to be while you enjoy telling all your friends what you have been up to! Another major ingredient of balanced Fire energy is, in fact, the ability to enjoy community, to enjoy "being with people." This can be facilitated by accepting people for who they are, meeting them with openness, tolerance, maybe forgiveness, and

*

Making positive changes to your space is fun! So spend time reveling in the positive side of life.

treating them with unconditional compassion, kindness, and love. This is not always an easy proposition, and it is made infinitely more difficult in a space with only one chair, one cup, one place to sit and eat food that only you like, and so on.

So, undertake a quick Feng Shui appraisal of your interior space, and see how well it works to encourage friendship and communication. Is there anywhere in your house that is set up for groups of people to enjoy? Lack of space is no excuse—we all remember a great occasion or gathering at one time in our lives that was set up in a space with the dimensions of a largish linen cupboard!

Take a good look around your space, starting in the hall, and ending in the bathroom, and experience it as if you are a guest visiting your home for the first time. How welcoming is the single coat hook, filled by your jacket, or the chairs placed so that two people can't sit comfortably and chat? How good do you feel when you walk into the kitchen and see a single box of teabags placed by a just enough mugs for the household and a solitary spoon? Think about the places you have been to that just shouted "great social life, loads of friends and good times" at you and see if you can remember any of the signals that made you believe it. Perhaps you will recall that there was a certain lack of rigidity, plenty of evidence of ongoing activities (a pile of tennis rackets, a bunch of glasses on a tray), a selection of places immediately available to sit in, a selection of drinks and cups in the kitchen, photos of friends enjoying life propped up on top of an open piano, a view through the window of a barbecue, table, and chairs.

> Undertake a quick Feng Shui appraisal of your interior space, and see how well it works to encourage friendship and communication.

Living with other people

Living with other people involves more than the household—make your home welcoming to all comers. Be ready to lay out food for an impromptu party.

Once you have spent some time reading the signals about your own Fire energy that your space is giving out, you will begin to realize how much good you can do yourself by working on this element alone. By being ruthlessly honest about your own willingness to open your heart, and your door, to the rest of humanity (or even just a chosen few) you will have a fairly good indication of the state of the level of your chi called Shen.

Spirituality doesn't have much to do with the erection of an altar at the disused end of a room in which the curtains are always closed, and no voice is heard except for your own. Nor does it have much to do with placing pictures of angels above an empty fireplace which is never the focus of a social group. One of the best ways to space clear a room (see pages 66–7), has always been to throw a party, with lots of children and animals on the guest list, and then to serve breakfast the next morning to all those who

stayed the night. This is an excellent way to boost the Fire energy of a space and its occupants, just as long as you leave the space time to settle down before the next burst of action arrives!

If you see every day as an opportunity to learn something more about yourself from the people around you, then you will find that living together as a family plays an important role in the cultivation of Shen, or spirit. With this end in mind, creating areas where the family can spend time together is a really valuable contribution to the good Feng Shui of a house. Aim to create space where people can actively participate in life together on reasonably equal terms, in other words, spaces that are safe, functional, and hospitable for a range of ages, abilities, and talents. You will find that places that are designed for "doing things in" are more life-enhancing than spaces that are designed to be looked at. It is, after all, far easier to learn to live with other people if one person isn't constantly preoccupied by the fear that the others will spoil their creative interior design statements. If you recognize yourself here, aspire to a measure of respect and love from all family members toward their communal living space, but try and find some other outlet for your creative talent.

Cultivating Fire energy isn't just about sharing your life with other people, but this is a sure way to learn some central lessons from life that will allow your spirit to flourish. Of course, knowing when you need to be alone, and creating space for that too, is an important part of the whole picture, and the only true way to create an overall balance. That is the seed of yin within yang, or the Water held still within the steadily burning Fire.

Don't aim for a home that is designed for a lifestyle of constant partying, simply one that allows for that possibility for some of the time. Your home, and life, should be able to accommodate many permutations, from one person and their quiet solitude, to a small group eating together, or a whole group actively enjoying their day. It is this sense of balance that will contribute to the good health of both you and your family.

*

Arrange your space so both the lively and the contemplative sides of life are catered for—space for lots of people, and spaces for just one.

Home and Office

Let us look at the ways in which we can rekindle our own personal inner Fire, our own Heart energy.

Anyone who is having difficulty feeling very generous or warm hearted to the people around them probably isn't having a very good time themselves. It is common for people who have an imbalance in their Fire energy to suffer from low self-esteem, or a lack of confidence in themselves, which can sometimes be expressed as the inability to see good in others. This can create havoc in the workplace.

Feelings of low self-esteem are often coupled with a symptomatic inability to feel recognized or acknowledged for our unique talents and skills by the community or the wider society in which we live. Again, this can cause some interesting office politics.

So how can we get that Fire to burn a little brighter and rekindle our love of ourselves, which will, in turn, just make us light up the whole area around us and get us noticed? Assuming that you have paid good attention to your space, as outlined in the previous pages, you can now go on to make some basic, fun changes that will act like a real "pick me up"!

Start by adding "all things shiny" to your main living room or office space. Silks and satins can bring with them a flurry of red and orange; they can be draped like flames of color, or they can burn steady and low as cushions. Curtain poles wound with red satin can replace heavy drapes or blinds, startlingly bright orange muslin hung around window frames will bring the whole room alive with energy. Glass tables will speed your energy right up; put one in your office for a desk and you can dispense with caffeine altogether! You will find that a glass coffee table, set with a triangular vase full of tiger lilies or

So how can we get that Fire to burn a little brighter and rekindle our love of ourselves, which will, in turn, just make us light up the whole area around us and get us noticed?

those stunningly exotic bird of paradise flowers, will bring power to any meeting, be it social or business.

Oil wood until it glows and hums, especially red woods like mahogany or cherry, and then replace your lampshades with ones that shine. Banish blue, purple, or white shades altogether, and buy some red candles to boost light levels in gloomy corners. Move to south-facing rooms (you will find a move to a south-facing window will make or break a grumbling employee). Find spaces with big windows that sit low in the walls and add window seats cushioned in cerise and scarlet, or even red PVC. If you really feel in need of a boost, add a gilt-framed mirror or two and watch your room, and life, take off.

Fire time is the time for action, courage, and daring. It is a time to bask in that high energy, make an impact, and enjoy being the talk of the town. However, if you or your colleagues or guests begin to get a little too high, a little too passionate, (verging on the hysterical) in your space, ease back a little. The first things to remove are the mirrors!

> You will find that a glass coffee table, set with a triangular vase full of tiger lilies or those stunningly exotic birds of paradise flowers, will bring power to any meeting, be it social or business.

Expanding into the space outside

Never underestimate the power of the space outside your home or office; it could save your Fire from going out completely. Using it effectively will make you blossom. All spaces have windows, and you should have windows that can be opened and that you can see out of easily. Always keep your windows sparkling clean, and open them all regularly. Try to have window boxes, or hanging baskets whenever possible—I have seen some spaces in tiny narrow streets that are festooned with plantlife. Flat roofs are just crying out to be made into roof gardens, and balconies can transform a space.

I once did a consultation for a thriving business that had created a wonderful rooftop garden that could be seen right down the street. It was the biggest asset of the space. When they moved into bigger premises, they managed to transform their office into one of the most high profile, high flying buildings that I have ever seen outside of a capital city. This time, a huge wraparound rooftop terrace and orchard boosted the Fire of their now multinational enterprise. The message here is that you should opt for expansion and display, like the male peacock who makes himself splendid by occupying as much space as possible, and in the most spectacular and remarkable way.

If nothing else, put up a shiny brass plaque announcing yourself on your office door, or put a fire-shaped

Place lights throughout your garden to invite Fire into the space—the more light you have, the more Fire you will attract.

If you are lucky enough to have some really useful outside space, make sure that you give it a facelift, and use absolutely every last corner of it.

light on your boundary line, just to push your energy out into the world a little more. If you are lucky enough to have some really useful outside space, make sure that you give it a facelift, and use absolutely every last corner of it. Make it a challenge to work out how to activate even the gloomiest, and most infertile, spots. Consider creating height in the garden; you don't need to have trees if you would prefer a pergola, an arched walkway, or a magnificent roofed seat or summerhouse, (open to the south side, naturally).

Whether you have children of your own or not, it is a good idea to introduce some opportunities to play, or at least be active into your backyard—try importing a jungle gym or watch tower. Animals and birds will do a lot to activate chi in a space, but it is better still to find yourself really using a garden, rather than just looking at it. By introducing a greenhouse, some distance from the house, you will be encouraged to grow things, even if it's just a grape vine or peach tree that wouldn't survive outside and needs lots of visits to keep it happy. Some glass in a garden is good—cold frames are ideal if space is limited, but they don't always work well with smaller children.

Remember, using a garden right through the year is important if you want to keep your Fire energy in balance during Winter and Autumn too.

A garden should be multifunctional, with areas for growing plants, playing, sitting still, and partying. Think carefully about introducing aspects of all the elements so that your garden can be used all year round.

Yoga
Practicing Yoga Outside and Konatadasana

> "The Yogi sees himself in the heart of all beings, and all beings in his heart."
>
> Bhagavad Gita

*

Feel your ankles open and strengthen as the soles of your feet reach into the ground.

What better way of being active in the garden than by taking your yoga mat and cushions and moving outside for your yoga practice? If you choose some even ground, you can dispense with your mat completely for the standing postures and enjoy letting the shape of the ground work your feet and ankles even more than usual.

There are a few guidelines to follow when you practice outside, but personally I think it is the best way to practice whenever you can.

• Practice in the shade and stick to morning or evening time, if there is hot sun.

• Make sure you always protect yourself, particularly your back, from chilly winds or cold.

• Orient yourself to face the sun when standing, and have your back to it when seated or lying down.

• Place your mat on perfectly dry ground.

For this summer, Fire practice, I suggest you choose a couple of favorite postures from each of the first two sections to practice before you move into these dynamic stretches. Try practicing these before you move outside if you find it easier.

Asana 1 Wide-legged Standing, or Konatadasana.

Practice this fantastically simple posture whenever you want to give your Fire chi a boost.

1. start by standing for a few moments in Tadasana—feet parallel, a hip width apart, shoulders dropped, and legs strong.

2. take some time to tune into your breathing and become aware of your feet against the ground. This is the feeling that you will refer to when you move into the next posture, so take some time to experience the way your weight is balanced over your feet and your ankles move strongly

upward, taking energy up into your legs, through your knees, and your pelvis into your body. Be aware of your chin being slightly dropped and the back of your neck long.

3. when you feel quite centered and "present," with your attention in your body, either step, or jump, your feet apart. Open your arms, being careful to place your feet with care and land lightly. Your energy should feel as though it is being carried up through your body and out of the top of your head. As you are standing be aware of letting your shoulders drop, your heartline—at the front and the back of your body—opening, and the palms of your hands tingling with life.

4. use your expanding breath to allow your arms to stretch out away from your body, as your weight lifts up out of your hips and you enjoy the feeling of your chi growing.

Keep your face directed forward throughout, your jaw relaxed, and your neck long.

The affirmation for this asana is 'My energy is expanding'.

Your shoulders will drop as your energy lifts through your body.

Virabhadrasana

Start as you mean to go on, beginning this asana with a mental assertion of confidence and power.

Virabhadra is a hero of Hindu legend; you need to feel open and strong to do this dynamic asana justice. This posture works directly to strengthen feet and legs, while opening the hips.

To begin, spend a few moments standing in Tadasana. This is translated as "Mountain" posture, so consider the quality of quiet strength that a mountain enjoys as you practice this fundamental asana. Notice also the apparent stillness in the context of vivid energy, (Fire) within, and enjoy the contrast between this asana, when the fire burns within stillness, and Virabhadrasna, when the fire leaps up and burns brightly right through to the periphery of the body. The secret of balanced Fire chi lies in the ability to remain calm and effortlessly contain this huge movement from embers to blaze.

1. to move into Virabhadrasana, either jump or step your feet apart, the distance of one of your wide strides, or a good step and a half. Your base should remain stable, with all four corners of both feet in easy contact with the floor, and your ankles lifting away strongly. Notice how it feels to stand with your feet so wide apart and be aware of breathing energy up through the ground into your legs and up through your torso. At this stage in the asana it is important that you try to establish a feeling of strength and wellbeing.

2. rotate one leg out—your foot will need to move so that it too is turned out to the side. As you do this the other foot can turn toward it slightly.

3. now you are ready to move into the full asana. Taking a deep breath in, feel your body expand and lift skyward, before breathing out and allowing the knee of the turned-out leg to bend and your arms to lift to the sides. The turn-out comes entirely from the hips; your knee should stay directly over your foot at all times.

4. you can allow your shoulders to drop; the life pumping through the center of your body will maintain the position of your arms, which stretch out to the sides. It is as though your arms extend because they must to allow your power full expression.

5. your body weight is carried by both legs, while you call upon the strength carried in your legs to support this wide and powerful position. It should feel as though you are growing in size and power with every breath.

Notice that your feet, especially the back foot, may feel compromised and you may feel the urge to peel it away from the floor. Don't give in, because if you do, the whole asana will be undermined!

Keep alert in the back foot and corresponding arm; it will help to balance the asana.

Wide-Legged forward bend

If the top of your head and the soles of your feet meet the floor you will feel the power of letting go.

There is no commonly recognized Sanskrit name for this posture that I have ever come across, and I have only occasionally found this asana taught, but I have always found it an invaluable posture used in tandem with the Virabhadrasana posture (see page 116–17), or on its own when it is hard to achieve complete relaxation by any other means. Often it is only when one can completely relax and "let go" that there follows a surge of energy or power that can come in physical or mental form.

To practice this asana, which is a great tonic for the heart, in tandem with the preceding two can be extremely invigorating.

You can rest in Tadasana or seated on the floor before moving into this asana if it feels right for you, otherwise move directly into it, enjoying the way this and the preceding asana combine. You can alter the position of the arms at different times.

Let's just run through the various arm position before we proceed.

• If your shoulders feel tight it is good to use the position with the hands linked behind your back, rotating them over your head as you move forward. You are aiming to create a feeling of space through your shoulders, neck, and upper back. Only move your arms while the elbows can remain straight and your neck relaxed.

• If you want to open the front of your chest and stretch your wrists use the position with your arms in namaste, "reverse prayer," or simply fold them behind your back if that feels better for you.

• Keep your hands tucked into your hip bone if you want to give your back more support and help focus your awareness on keeping a strong abdomen.

Once you have chosen you preferred arm positions, check the contact with the ground that your feet are making. Bend forward as though you were hinged at the hip, keeping your back long and your abdomen strong. Also be aware of the work that your inner thighs will have to do to keep the posture alive. There should be no feeling of collapse; your ankles and feet need to work and keep "present" in the posture and your hips

should open to let your body through and forward. Allow your head to drop and release all its weight downward.

There will be a sense of energy flowing up from the ground, up through your legs and then moving unimpeded through your spine on its journey back towards the ground.

Try to imagine unwanted chi, in the form of thoughts, responsibilities, anxiety, or stress flowing freely out of your head and into the floor as you exhale. If you have long hair, the image is all the easier! All the while fresh chi, life, is being drawn up from the very center of the earth through your feet and ankles and into your body each time you inhale. If you can spend a little time in the asana, you will begin to feel this wonderful cleansing and invigorating rhythm pulsing through your whole being.

*

Perform this asana with your arms in namaste and the sacred geometry you create will sound a prayer.

Vrksasana

The affirmation for this asana is "My mind is at rest."

Vrks is Sanskrit for "tree." This asana must be included in this summer/Fire section because it is such a wonderful way to focus the mind and bring clarity into the moment. You may find that on some days it is an absolute demon to practice, being elusive and infuriating and perplexing all at once. On other days it is your best friend—steady, stoic, and reliable. On those days it will make you want to smile, or grin, or even laugh out loud. It is the ideal asana to help you cultivate Fire energy and, like Tadasana, it liberates that flame from a place of containment and inner calm.

Try to practice this asana somewhere really beautiful outside. If you get the chance, go somewhere with big

*

Allow your hips to open and your breath to flow freely as the top of your head reaches skyward.

horizontal energy, where the eye can see for miles and the spirit can just keep on expanding and expanding. Try practicing with a friend, and that burst of Fire will be filling you with laughter and light heartedness within minutes. Once you have experienced your chi kicking into life and expanding enough to make you grin while standing there balanced on one leg, you will be an absolute addict. You can't fall into the trap of taking yourself too seriously while practicing this asana, and I guarantee that, if you did, for even a moment, you would lose your balance!

Incidentally, the key to balance is to keep both the straight and folded leg alive and working hard, stretch up out of your hips, and keep your body moving around your breath. As soon as you become static and start "holding on" to the pose, the whole thing will just die. You may remain upright, but you will not feel the rush of opening chi—the whole reason for practicing this asana. (You can acquire strong legs by simply going to the gym!)

So, begin, as ever, in Tadasana.

1. when you feel ready, fold one leg so that your foot is tucked up into your groins, in either of the two variations shown. In both cases make sure that the turnout comes from the hip, and isn't just happening at the knee or ankle. The hips should remain facing front and level; there is no need to allow any twisting into the pelvis.

2. allow yourself a few breaths to adjust to this position before either deciding to stay with this stage of the asana, or moving on.

3. if you are going to move on, begin by bringing the palms of your hands together, so that your fingers first meet just below your navel, then moving them up along the center line of your body.

4. you may either complete the asana here, with your hands by your breastbone, or continue to lift them skyward, opening them as they move above your head.

5. you will want to stand and enjoy the full and complete power and clarity this asana brings before slowly and carefully retracing your steps back to Tadasana.

Karma Yoga

The joy discovered in simply sitting still, in the awareness of your physical body and spiritual self—this tranquillity can be incorporated into your daily life.

For this fifth asana of the summer/Fire chi section of this book, I want to suggest that you do something that will take you to the heart of your own story. Take your own experience of yoga to date out beyond the confines of your yoga mat and into your life!

During the practice of Karma Yoga, without even being conscious of it, the student takes their awareness of themselves, the way their energy is carried in the body, their breath, their contact with the ground and with the sky, into their daily life. By doing this, they aim to cultivate their awareness of their connection to all other parts of the universe, or in Taoist philosophy terms, they aim to cultivate Shen (our sense of our spirit or of our heart).

By practicing the yoga asanas we can begin to experience the one unity of which everything is a part because we have heightened our sense of ourselves by being acutely aware of, for example, the way our feet are on the ground, our breath, how our chi is flowing through our body, how our mind and senses are being affected by our physical bodies. As we become accustomed to this heightened sense of awareness, we can take it into other parts of our lives.

Here are some of the practical suggestions that I have been using over the years to help people take the heart of their asanas with them into their day.

The affirmation for this asana is "I am at the heart of all things, and all things rest in my heart."

- Walk barefoot for some of the time every day.
- Abandon sitting on chairs completely for a day; after that only sit on them when you have to. Give your hips a treat and sit on the floor instead.
- Practice relaxing by slowly breathing in through your nose and out through your mouth every time you begin to feel a familiar response to stress, thereby telling your body it is safe to stay open and strong.
- Relax your face and let your mask drop every time you feel resistance to doing something, then you may be able find another way to do it.
- Next time you are running, or participating in your favorite sport, do it just as though it was a yoga asana and watch the difference it makes.

The Crow/Kakasana

Everyone calls this asana "the Crow," because it helps to make sense of the way the body feels when practicing it. It is a strange, often neglected posture, and is guaranteed to lighten the mood of even the most serious yoga class.

Its execution has something to do with strength in the arms and wrists, which is certainly built by practicing this asana, but it also has a lot to do with maneuverability, and the preparedness to adopt unfamiliar shapes. It concentrates the mind wonderfully, while reminding us that we are only souls with a shape to carry us for all our posturing and preening!

As an asana it will gather your energy back in after a session of wide and expansive Fire poses, while fine tuning that high summer chi before you roll up your yoga mat for the day.

The key to balance is strength, agility, and moving breath. Allow a smile to help all three.

When you first practice it, place a bundle of cushions in front of you; lots of people topple forward when first playing with this asana! It may help you to loosen up your hips with some of the wintertime/Water chi postures for the hips before you begin.

1. begin by squatting down on the ground with your feet wider than your hips. It doesn't matter if your heels are not on the ground, and it helps to turn your legs/feet out slightly.

2. lean forward to place the palms of your hands securely on the ground directly in front of you, shoulder width apart. Your hands are now your feet, so feel the palms of your hands become the soles of your feet and your fingers, your toes.

3. drop your hips and give your back a good stretch as you extend forward to meet the ground full on with your hands.

4. at this point, spend some time gently rocking your weight backward and forward, getting very comfortable with the idea of moving your center of gravity forward over your hands. Keep your wrists strong, they will behave like your ankles, pulling chi up through the palms of your hands and up into your legs. Your arms push back against your legs, allowing your body to move through the space and to a position with your chest open and your head extended well forward.

5. as you approach the furthest point of the asana imagine the crow cawing, giving voice. This visualization, or actual sounding, helps to move chi from the base chakra of your body through your solar plexus, chest, and throat. It helps to you to create the forward impetus to achieve the balanced position that you are moving toward.

Emotional Wellbeing
Suspending Judgement

Do you immediately know, with barely a moment needed for consideration, the answers to these three questions?

• How well did you do yesterday?

• How much better could you do today?

• Based on the above two answers, how much better can you realistically expect to do tomorrow?

And now select from the possible answers below, a response to this final question;

• How hard are you on yourself?

Answer:

• Unbearably, cruelly hard.

• Fairly hard—I need to be or my life would just fall apart

• Ridiculously hard, and slightly harder when life isn't going well!

Most of us have been brought up believing that, because in some way we are naturally lazy, greedy, self-indulgent, and altogether not terribly bright, we have to make up for all these inadequacies by keeping a very firm hold on all our natural tendencies. If they are given free rein they might lead us to a life of self-indulgence,

Allowing yourself to be yourself outside the constraints you place will make you happier, freer, and more able to love and be loved.

sloth, and nonachievement. This whole belief structure is at the root of the "fear-driven" behavior, stress, anger, and lack of self-esteem that makes us so unhappy.

But if you could just spend one hour doing exactly as you pleased, and then another, and another, you would, in time, and after a little practice (and, of course, the initial panic-stricken strange behavior of an animal uncaged for the first time), begin to realize that you are a person worth having a little faith in. And if you can have faith in yourself, who knows what may happen to your relationships with the people around you?

Affirmations that will improve your relationships all around are:

- "I am perfect just the way I am" (Yes I know it may feel risky to say, or even think!)
- "I am just where I need to be in my life right now"
- "I can reveal my power and still be loved"

Hiding your true potential

Have you ever wondered why all your dreams don't come true? Have you ever felt that you have never quite blossomed in the way you knew you could? Or have you ever simply wondered why people just don't seem to recognize or acknowledge you for all you can do?

My guess is that you have been unconsciously, systematically, and habitually hiding your light, dumbing down, holding yourself in a little, or a lot, in order to stay safe and survive. But how can keeping your power largely hidden from the world around you keep you safe, or help you to survive?

We all come into the world absolutely in full command of our power. Our individuality shines brightly out for all to see and experience, but the people around us may find it problematical to deal with this vibrancy. We are too happy, (or too sad), too alert, too ready to tell it as it really is, too keen to question and wonder and be prepared to really "go for it" in every way, every moment of the day. Sadly, in too many cases, we are met with a less than positive response.

The joy and vibrancy we see in children was once ours too—and all it takes is a little practice to rediscover this in ourselves.

We make people feel uncomfortable by forcing them to confront the person that they really are, and the sort of life that they have created for themselves. We may be expressing parts of ourselves that they have been unable to cope with in themselves. We are "too much responsibility," "too hot to handle," "too difficult," or just "too time consuming." Unwittingly, we cause havoc.

And this is where, at a tender age, our survival instincts kick in. We quickly learn that if we appear a little less bright, a little less in command of every atom of our power and potential, we will be giving our carers an easier time, and they will shower us with the rewards of acceptance, love, and nurturing. So, on a very basic level, hiding our light, keeping large parts of ourselves hidden, becomes the key to our survival.

We are clever enough to learn acceptable ways of behavior, often by guessing what our carers expect of us and providing them with just that. Much of the time we are expected to "fit in" with other people, to keep them comfortable, rather than put them into a position where they may have to feel more, take more responsibility for their lives, or possibly even change!

All of these ways of behaving suppress who we really are, and everything that is really vital, different, and unique to us. By the time we reach the age when we are no longer dependent on our carers' approval, the pattern is already well set.

At about this time you might wonder, "what happened to the real me, where did I go, where has all my confidence gone, why is my self-esteem so low, why does nobody acknowledge me for my true self, my true worth?"

The lack of confidence in ourselves and our decisions is a side effect of the control we have learned to have over our emotions in order to make those around us feel comfortable. Releasing ourselves will enable us and our loved ones to be free to experience the joys life has to offer.

Make your dreams come true

Have you done too good a job of "fitting in," toning yourself down, becoming acceptable? Hiding your light, and all the associated behavior and life patterns that you have created for yourself to help you to do this, could damage or limit you, and everybody that you come into contact with. Once you allow yourself to express your full potential, you will begin to see how you are inviting the people around you to take stock of their own positions, to heal themselves, and maybe give themselves permission to shine a little more brightly too!

So, how do you go from being a little ember tucked into the corner of the hearth with all the other little embers, to being a great hearty blaze?

STEP ONE

Give a great blast of gratitude to your carers for allowing you to survive in a strong enough way to be able to be taking this huge step forward now!

STEP TWO

Acknowledge the wonderful qualities about yourself that you can use to build on, and make a mental list of at least five things you do really well—anything from knowing how to really enjoy a good shower, to being able to know just what to say to a friend in need. Celebrate these things and decide to add to this list every single day. Self-esteem is about action, not words.

STEP THREE

Think about someone in your group of friends or acquaintances who you consider to be publicly successful, high profile, and confident in themselves. Then think about someone else with similar qualities. Begin to learn from other people by looking at the way they relate to

*

Enhancing you Fire chi and allowing yourself to be full of joy and confidence is a skill that can be learned with just a little practice.

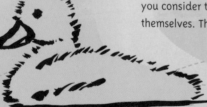

themselves and other people. What do they consistently expect for themselves? What do they consistently receive? How do they consistently treat the people around them? (The real successes in life are those who are generous and nonjudgmental to themselves and others.)

STEP FOUR

Cast your mind back to any little, (or big!), fantasies you used to have about what you might have wanted to do—things that you never actually did for one reason or another. Notice what stopped you and see if you can use this information as a clue to picking up a thread of a part of yourself that you have lost.

STEP FIVE

Risk revealing the totality of "you." Dress to look fabulous, not acceptable. Speak to express your real thinking, not what you think other people want to hear. Behave as though everything is possible for you, not as though you know your limits.

Food
Food and Energetics

When I began researching this part of the book, I looked first at the classic texts from the East. These, of course, led directly to the macrobiotic approach to food, and from there to texts on healing foods, on herbs (both Eastern and Western), to the numerous volumes on eating to cure specific ailments, to detox, and thence to the wonderful array of books written by all those Fire-type people who seem to live exotic and appealing lives, and who share recipes for appetizers, main courses, and desserts.

When prepared and eaten with love food can be a spiritual source of chi.

The yawning gap that emerged in all the reading and research was that, beyond the cacophony of voices clamoring to "eat this," or "don't at any cost eat this," there was very little understanding of the most crucial part of the whole business of food and eating—the energetic component of food. This elusive part of the process is almost entirely neglected. Eating food in such a way that one is able to cultivate Fire chi, for example, involves more than just the choice of ingredients. We have talked about the process of choosing and gathering ingredients already, and gone on to discuss the ways in which we "cook our energy into our food." Now we can fully appreciate the dynamic that occurs when we take on new life in the form of food. We can do that as part of our study of Fire chi.

In the following pages I want to bring our focus away from the current recipe-driven approach to food, away even from the "check the label" approach!

Having plowed through numerous texts urging me to only eat obscure green vegetables, a wide variety of grains, (does any one you know eat millet, for example, on a regular basis, or at all?), and to indulge my desire for the sensuous with some porridge oats drizzled in rice syrup, I have come away discouraged and irritable enough to give up entirely on ever eating again.

*

Food can be for the soul as well as the body.

Most of us know what we should be eating and why, and compromise with the "so long as its fresh and chemical free, press the go button" approach to eating most of the time. Let's abandon the recipe mentality and look at food designs instead and commit to thinking, for a while, about the energetics of our food and eating.

Finding a positive approach to food

When we talk about energetics and summer/Fire chi, we are talking about finding ways of eating that make us feel more warm and expansive, more confident, expressive, and convivial. All of these feelings can be enhanced by the ways in which we gather the ingredients, prepare, and then eat them.

In practical terms you do have a choice about how you gather ingredients together. Do you want to do this alone, or with someone else? Where would be a really nurturing place to go to shop, somewhere that would make you feel alive and joyful? Or maybe you feel that you have lost those choices. How would it alter your approach to food, and the way you cooked and ate it, if you started the process in the most positive way possible?

The planning, buying, and preparing of food can be fun and add to the whole experience. Sharing food with those we love is one part of the experience.

> Remember, small quantities of delicious things bursting with aroma and sensuousness have got to be a better way to start a fire than a bulk purchase of something you didn't think you wanted until you saw it was "on special."

Start right now to consider how the very experience of thinking about food can begin to feed you.

If you are focusing on Fire chi, then you might find that you would like to go and shop somewhere theatrical—this could be the seashore to buy fish, a fantastic baker's with a coffee shop for bread, or a covered market alive with the smell of cheeses, flowers, and fruit.

Food designs

Now that the business of shopping has begun to make you feel good, (I hope that everyone could think of at least one way to improve the experience), you will be feeling more loving toward the food that you have brought into your home. So, build on the love, and select a wonderful venue for the eating part.

A simple rule for building Fire chi, is to always eat every meal, breakfast included, outside! If that's not possible, at least throw open windows or doors, let the outside say hello to the inside, and if possible, occasionally take everything lock, stock, and barrel far away outside, and picnic.

The next simple rule for building Fire chi, is to eat with friends whenever you can. If you don't already have the outside and picnic habit,

*

The way you eat your food is as important as what you eat. Eating leisurely with friends outside in the summer is the perfect way to allow joyful Fire chi into all your lives.

develop it quickly! There is no better Fire tonic than fabulous food, great company, (even if it is only the dog or a good book; needs must!), eaten somewhere really staggeringly beautiful. Think about choosing the location, setting the stage, and calling up the cast.

One great way of building Fire chi in the winter months is to find a place to build a huge log fire and gather around it, wrapped up and exotic in your winter finery, to eat and drink and delight in the elements coming together in such a powerful and invigorating way.

Food Designs, unlike recipes, look at the whole eating, self-recreating, package, and extend to shopping, gathering ingredients and people, finding the perfect place, and looking after the way you feel about the whole business of eating. This is a very fluid and creative way to approach food, and respects our need for spontaneity, as well as our need for structure.

Food Designs put food back in perspective, and make people smile! They are about lifestyle, not just about eating, and they are about the way we change our energy around eating and the way we can recreate ourselves in any way that we wish.

The Food Design for a summer picnic might read,

Location: foot of green hill under old oak

Time: at the resting time of the day, after exercise and work

Company: two family groups, children's friends, associated dogs!

Essential food and drink items: pitted black olives brought back from vacation, ciabatta bread, cheeses, sardines from local deli, apricots from friends' garden, salad from ours, fresh mint for tea, elderflower cordial, friends' homemade cake, walnut loaf from new bakery in town.

Optional food and drink: anything that takes our fancy when packing hampers.

Essential additional items: large rugs, (three), daily newspapers to share, towel (someone always falls in the stream!), dogs' water bowl, baseball bat and soft ball (numerous uses!).

Other Essentials: people happy to share carrying the hamper, prepared to help stop the dogs from worrying the sheep, happy to sleep in the sun to give the children time and space to play.

4

Earth Transience

Transformation

Think of yourself for a moment as an Earthling. The Earth is the place where you have been born, your planet, and your friend. Your soul has chosen this physical human form, this place to be, and so, in this sense, you are of the Earth. You walk the space between Heaven and Earth, between the polar opposites of yang (chi raining down on you from the breadth of the heavens) and yin (chi growing out toward you from the center of the Earth, from a place of beginning that is beyond the limits of the Earth itself). It is at the point of meeting, at the moment of fusion between yin and yang, that energy is released to create new life. The Earth itself can be seen as the product of the same process, the result of the fusion of yang and yin, the meeting of the movement out from the center, and in from the widest reaches of the universe. In this way we share our own make-up with our planet, and are innately connected to it. However, in order for this huge dynamic to successfully complete, and give way to life, there needs to be a mediating mechanism, a gearing system or pivot. Without this maintenance of

*

Just like the Earth, you need to embody yin and yang within yourself, letting it flow effortlessly through your life, working with your life force, not against it.

> The Earth itself can be seen as the result of the fusion of yang and yin, the meeting of the movement out from the center, and in from the widest reaches of the universe.

*

The Earth is our home, it is the place that nurtures us and provides for us. The Earth element too is the caring element in the cycle, a haven from the changes life throws at us.

balance, the creative impulse would be dissipated.

This role is fulfilled by Earth chi, and its manifestation is the Earth, and all the physical life that is present on this planet. So, there is a direct connection between Earth chi, and the Earth itself, and even the earth that we walk on and dig and grow things in. Looking at all these things can help us to come closer to understanding the role of Earth chi in the five element cycle.

As you look at the position of Earth chi in the cycle you will see that it is traditionally placed between Fire, in seasonal terms high summer, and Metal, in seasonal terms, autumn. It is sometimes given a seasonal name, for the sake of tidiness and to introduce some notion of its transitional, balancing role in the energetic, or yearly and seasonal cycles. But I think that, in order to make real sense, and use, of the concept of Earth chi, it is worth taking the theoretical explanation one step further and looking at one of the charts used by students and practitioners of Feng Shui. This is a really good starting point for our understanding of the value and huge significance of Earth chi in our lives and will demystify what can become rather an obscure and mysterious concept.

Transformation

If you look at the chart illustrating the movement of chi through time and space, you will notice that we have moved from a position in which the elements appear once each, as they did in the chart on page 7, progressing in a creative cycle that reflects the movement of the seasons during the course of a year. Now we can see the elements waxing and waning, moving, for example, between small (less) Wood to big (more) Wood, and small (less) Metal to big (more) Metal. Fire and Water remain unchanged. Earth retains its original position in the creative cycle, between Fire and Metal and appears twice more, once at the center, and once between Water and Wood.

This chart, however, takes us beyond a representation of the way in which chi is created in time and adds a spatial dimension. If we use it in its simplest form, as shown here, it is easy to see how it represents the balancing, gearing role of Earth as we move from a time and place where yin dominates (when the impetus of yin is most determining in the creating and manifesting process), to a time and place where yang is dominating (when the impetus of yang is most determining in the creative and manifesting process). It is at that moment, when Wood chi rises and gives birth to a new day, a new year, that there is a huge shift of energy. This energy is moved into a position of creativity, rather than chaos, by the centering, balancing role of Earth. Again, when summer must give way to autumn, the height of midday to the falling energy of the afternoon, Earth comes into play to help negotiate the transformation.

If you look at this chart you will see that beyond these two positions, Earth also holds a central location, to represent that it is central to all things, and that all great movements across the range are mediated by Earth. I have also added reference to the spatial dimension which forms part of our understanding of the nature of chi. You will see that Earth occupies the locations that are manifestations of chi from the northeast, the center and the southwest. You may have noticed also that the remaining directions fall

The Earth element provides the foundation for the flowing energy levels at the center of all the elements.

This chart shows the way the elements, seasons, times of day, and compass directions combine to form a coherent whole.

logically into our existing understanding of the quality of chi present, for example, in the winter/Water part of the cycle. Reference to this chart will help to explain the role of placement in Feng Shui, and the use of directional energy to boost or drain the elements.

The reason that I have included this directional layer on the chart is that it makes clear that Earth occupies the whole of a diagonal running from northeast to southwest, showing the connection between these directions (or places) and times in the creative cycle when the effect of Earth is at its most powerful.

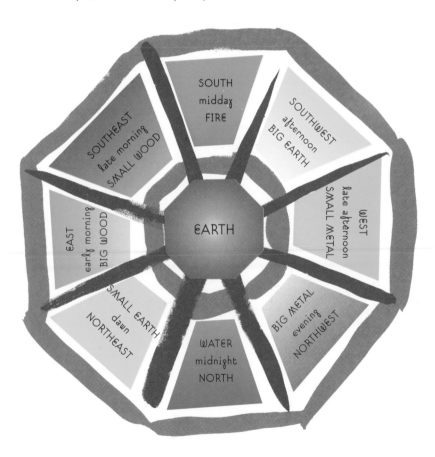

Transformation

*It is the Earth energy
that allows change
to occur in smooth
transitions. It holds
us in balance while
yin and yang fluctuate.*

Times of great change are volatile moments, and the directions (in which movement toward or out from the center is included), introduced on the previous page, share that same quality. They must be places where significant movement can be integrated and transformed in order to maintain the creative process, in order for life to continue.

So Earth energy needs to be fostered as a balancing, centering quality, enabling yin and yang to function within a creative process that constantly accepts death and allows life. As such, Earth energy forms an integral part of the smooth cyclical progression of creation in all its parts. It mediates and negotiates, without judgement or attachment, the transformation between matter, relying on strength at the center to create an axis on which the whole can turn.

The planet Earth shares the qualities of Earth chi, but is not in itself all that Earth chi is, in the same way that water shares qualities of Water chi, but the two are not one and the same. In order to nurture our own Earth chi, each of us needs to look to our sense of self, our center, emotionally, spiritually, and physically.

In Chinese medicine, the Earth element is said to govern the spleen, which is associated with the stomach, small intestine, and pancreas. The function of these parts is said to be integral to the distribution of all elements of food to the appropriate parts of the body. In other words, this function again concerns the transformation of matter (or chi) between manifestations (food, energy, waste products). The energy of plant or animal life is transformed into human form, and the mediating element is Earth. On a physical level an imbalance of Earth chi is often expressed as an excess, or depletion, of the flesh, or as a problem directly associated with the stomach or digestive system. Malfunction of the pancreas and associated problems such as diabetes, an impaired immune system, or anemia are all further indications of possible Earth chi imbalance. In terms of emotional health, being easily thrown off balance, particularly by other people, perhaps becoming overdependent, or giving ourselves to others to a debilitating degree, can all be indications that our Earth chi needs more support.

Nourishing ourselves and others appropriately and being able to recognize, and use, a whole range of resources for this purpose is the task of balanced Earth chi, and depends largely on the way in which we were ourselves nourished during our early life. Many of us

have the opportunity to really transform our lives by going back to our roots and assessing what we are drawing our energy from. By doing this, we will be able to evaluate what has been given to us to feed our center, our own self.

Earth energy mediates and negotiates, without judgement or attachment, the transformation between matter, relying on strength at the center to create an axis on which the whole can turn.

Going back to our roots

Enhancing Earth can help to remedy a lack of nurturing during childhood. It can nurture you as an adult, and the child within you.

During my years as a Feng Shui consultant, going out to look at people's homes and seeking to help them heal their lives, I have encountered the same set of circumstances over and over again. I have found that knowledge about Earth energy cures alone could help vast numbers of clients. It seemed an unfortunate fact that many of the people I saw would have benefited immensely had someone taken the time and care, and had the wisdom, to foster their Earth chi from their earliest moments, at least until that second great transformation at puberty.

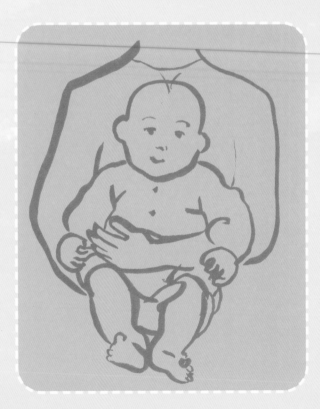

It is no coincidence that people talk about "earth mothers" when they want to convey an image of someone in touch with the creative process at its most earthy and practical. Time and time again when I am standing in someone's home I have a sense that I am involved in an attempt to remedy the past, or make up for a huge lack of nurturing. The business of being held emotionally, spiritually, and physically, and being appropriately nurtured is crucial to us if we are to be able to make the essential transitions through life.

With this in mind, take a look around your space as you consider the following question, which I have illustrated with a recent case study.

• Does your current space resemble in any way a space that you have lived in before, or in any way resemble a house in which you were brought up? Be careful here, sometimes the most obscure details are crucial.

I was recently at a consultation where the client had chosen her particular home almost purely because it had a garden. She had also chosen her bedroom because it opened onto the garden, furthermore, she spent a large part of her life in her bed which was oriented to look straight into the garden. Her friend commented on how uninterested in current life she was, and how overdependent she had become on herself, and on endlessly lying in bed. She was young, successful, and healthy, she just wanted to lie in bed all day.

When I asked her where she had been brought up, she responded that she had lived in a series of apartments in Hong Kong. There had, however, been a brief but idyllic period as a small child while her parents still lived together, that had been spent in a house with a garden. She initially forgot this crucial piece of information and I only discovered it after questioning her specifically about an image I saw of a small child being called in from a garden where she was playing happily. She was instinctively turning toward a time of happiness, when she was being nurtured by her parents, in an attempt to give herself the quality of life that she was currently lacking.

We often recreate situations, like my client, because we have unresolved issues. If we are still recreating issues from the past, a Feng Shui diagnosis would indicate that Earth chi was in need of support.

***

Earth chi is the strength on which all things rest; to gain strength for yourself you could seek to balance the Earth chi in your life.

Supporting Earth Chi

Recreating your childhood as an adult will not allow you to live in the present or grow into your future. Spot the signs and make changes.

Obviously, in the case of my client on the previous page, our task was to find another way of supporting her Earth chi, one that didn't involve lying in bed all day looking out onto a garden that had become a symbol of a time when she received the nurturing that she needed, but had not received in a very long time. Some of us, on the other hand, will go on recreating the same set of circumstances over and over again for other reasons, often because things weren't right the first time and we are trying to remedy the situation now.

All this may sound confusing, so here are some practical ways to help you to make sense of the Earth energy of your own space:

• Find out what lies directly southwest from the center of your home, or what is positioned in the southwest corner of your home. Look especially for neglected areas, collections of less than valuable objects, positive eyesores (often in the form of outbuildings, posts, or poles). Also look for similar obstructions in the top right-hand corner of your floor plan, when the position of the front door lies along the bottom edge of the plan.

• Observe the condition of your floors. Are they in a tiptop state, or something less than this? Do you find yourself obsessing about the state of the floors, or constantly repairing damage that seems to appear for no apparent reason?

• Check the boundary lines of your space. Are they clear and well defined or obscure, partial, or—even worse—a point of conflict between you and the outside world?

• Are you living in a space that you have duplicated from a previous occasion? Be careful, compare floor plans, including all land, boundary lines, gates, and outbuildings or significant items such as trees or ponds. It may be the wider location that is similar; for example, you may have lived more than once in a house that was built on land sloping from right to left, or in a

Having poorly supported Earth chi could reveal itself in broken boundaries, physical or emotional.

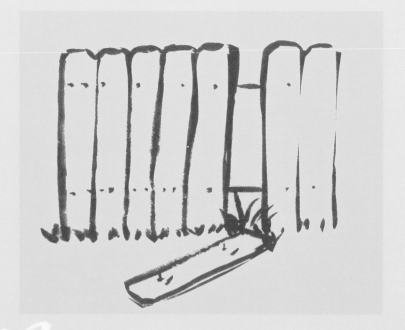

house with an open space immediately to the rear, even if on one occasion it was a field, on another a parking lot, and another time an empty house.

All these signs may be physical manifestations of Earth chi in need of support. You may be experiencing physical or emotional symptoms as well, and these can be numerous and varied, but a common theme may be digestive/food issues, sexual (as distinct from reproductive) difficulties, relationship difficulties, problems with mothering or being mothered.

Working to support Earth chi

If we can support the Earth chi of our space, then this will feed back to us, and help us to rebuild our foundations to become stronger and more centered. Careful monitoring of any Earth chi imbalance is certainly a step in the right direction, but it is easy enough to work more actively to promote Earth chi. One of the most powerful things that you can do is to repair, respect, and honor the Earth you walk on, and make it a pleasure to do so every time you come home. Keep your paths, floors, steps, and stairs in tiptop condition, as an affirmation of the metaphysical honoring of the ground we walk on and the way in which we make contact with and interface with our physical world. This can also be interpreted as the path we walk, the way we live our lives, the degree of respect we have for our planet, our community, and ourselves, and the connection between all these. By doing this, you will not only bring your center of attention down through the body, making you appreciate your physicality, you will find the firm foundations that you may have missed out on earlier on. Don't think about it, try it.

You should also clarify in your own mind where your boundaries are, then put something there so that everyone else knows too. Physical boundaries around your space, the limits of the space under your care, such as the boundary line of your land, or your front gate, act as a direct physical reflection of your internal personal boundaries. In the same way the extent of one's responsibilities for others, or the preparedness for putting one's own needs before another person's can be marked out.

Next, return to thinking about other spaces that you have lived in and take note of any replications of those spaces in your current home. Work out what these replications might mean to

Take the time to look at the environment you have created for yourself. See what it has to tell you about yourself, then gather your courage to make the changes that your heart tells you to make.

you and deal with any issues that they might raise. Treat all the things you notice as symbols and messages, banish disbelief, and be prepared to read the story that they are telling you. Ask what your space tells you about the following: How have you been nurtured? How well are you able to recognize and receive the resources this world has to offer? How strong a sense of self have you built? How easily can you feel secure enough to give appropriately to others?

If you have followed these points, and still feel seriously lacking in Earth energy, here are some more fantastic fixes to support your space, and yourself, further:

One of the most powerful things that you can do is to repair, respect, and honor the Earth you walk on, and make it a pleasure to do so every time you come home.

• Imagine how you would have chosen, designed, and arranged your space if you had had the mother, and mothering, of your dreams. Take your time, write your findings down, date and sign the paper, decide to implement the changes.

• Go to an interior design shop, buy paints the color of saffron, turmeric, amber, and cinnamon, add fabrics and light shades, and come home and play with adding them to the least homey part of your home.

• Find square-shaped or cube-shaped items, such as terra cotta tiles and solid tables, and add them to your home at ground level. Make windows square by the addition of blinds and scatter checked fabrics and gingham cloths around your home.

• Build a walled garden with only one gate, and plant it with box hedging and low-growing shrubs or plants. Add gravel paths and, if you have enough room, some sturdy little trees that you can sling a hammock between one day.

Earth chi for our children

*
Enhancing the Earth chi for your children means starting with yourself. Supporting the Earth chi throughout your home will automatically mean balancing Earth chi for you, and for your kids.

One of the ways in which we can discover what was lacking in our own childhood and how we can remedy it, is by watching what we give, or would like to give, to other people, especially our children. We tend to give our children the best of what was given to us, and more, but sometimes we overcompensate by giving things to our children that they neither want nor need, or by living out our own fantasies through them. The ways in which we relate to children can teach us a lot about ourselves, and help us to support ourselves in ways that help us and take the pressure off our kids too.

Providing spaces for our children that will support their own Earth Chi will have two positive results:

• They will grow up gracefully and securely.

• We will get less exhausted on a day-to-day parenting basis, because the environment will be doing some of the work for us.

The first step to take is to seriously consider all of the actions and ideas mentioned in the preceding chapters, and prioritize working on your own space and energy. You will need to do this before you even start to think about addressing the needs of your children, because they will almost certainly coincide with yours. In other words, your children share your issues, often expressing those that you cannot deal with for yourself.

Notice, for example, the duplication of design features/problems shared by your space and your child's room. This may be very obvious—you chose a house with small windows in every room, including your child's, or subtle—your bedroom door handle is always falling off, so is his. Make a list of shared features, read them like a story or set of signs and symbols, and use them to work out what is, and isn't, working in your life.

Now look at the things that your child loves about his space. Ask him, and give him plenty of time to answer. Sometimes you need to pose children questions in a number of different ways, and at different times, in order to access their feelings. Avoid a discussion based on "what I don't like" and find out about their priorities by building on the good.

Talk about other places that they've liked to sleep or play in. Behave as though their space matters, but bear in mind that, if children end up designing their whole room, or an entire color scheme, this may put them in too powerful and scary a position. You're just asking them for input, while staying in the responsible role.

More support for people, young and old

*

To strike the right balance to enhance your Earth chi requires creating a balance of your own. Your home need not be too cluttered, nor too empty.

When you are looking at your child's space you might want to plan any changes that you intend to make in advance, talking him/her through the process and taking it as slowly as your child needs. You will find that children are often more open to the effects of changes in chi than older people and it is important to observe the effects that the changes you are making to their space are having on them.

When parents are working with their children's space, they often complain that their children are hoarders, who won't let them throw anything away, and that they don't appreciate the new things that are bought for them, clinging instead to familiar old toys.

People also blame their partners for hoarding, and this can be one of the main barriers to rearranging space in a supportive way.

One of the keys to getting it right with Earth chi is to sort out the whole way you use resources; this will be clearly reflected back to you in the Feng Shui of your space. Could any of these terms be used to describe your space?

• Stark, cold, dark or gloomy, neglected, worn out, unfinished.

• Crammed full, bursting at the seams, not a square inch of space left.

Now answer the following questions:

• Have you always lived in a big house, but never heated it adequately?

• Do you still rely on one overhead light to light each room?

• Do you say no to luxuries and opportunities without even thinking?

• Do you have storage cupboards that you haven't seen the back of in months, or dare I say it, years?

• Do you stockpile absolutely anything, or specifically something (food or cosmetics)?

If you've answered "yes" to some of these questions, you may be one of those people who live on our wonderful planet and yet don't really feel that you deserve what it offers, or maybe you worry that if you have something it won't be there for someone else, or will run out. Maybe you don't really believe that you will be able to receive whatever you need when you need it, or that someone other than yourself might be there to notice your needs and look after them. So, you either stockpile or starve.

Stockpilers need to clutter-clear and practice trust.

People who starve themselves need to treat themselves, to surround themselves with the things they need, and practice trust. Ask yourself: What is the nature of trust for each one of us? How do we relate to and negotiate issues of trust?

Do we even recognize the need for trusting the life process with which we are involved?

Do we trust that all is well in the world and that whatever happens to us or comes our way, all will continue to be well, because the natural order of things is a good and fair one and designed to help us to learn and develop our true nature?

Do we trust people that we meet, live with, and are surrounded by?

Do we trust ourselves, or do we suspect ourselves of being intrinsically "bad" or out of control emotionally?

Asking these types of questions will lead us to the things that we need to address in our lives in order to live from a position of trust.

Do one thing every day that feels a bit risky—lose a bit of clutter that you think you may not be able to do without, or use up some of those hoarded resources to make your day (or moment) a little bit happier.

Learning to do without the things we hoard can be hard but it is worth having a clutter clear-out. Keep only what you need, dispense with clutter, and you free yourself to new exciting opportunities.

Yoga
Cobra

This is the first of a series of asanas that are specifically designed to support, strengthen, and open the center of the body. Strengthening your physical center will make you able to move with more confidence and freedom in a whole range of ways, from the ability to run and jump with ease to being able to perform actions that require strength and dexterity from the whole body. It also protects you from injury and maintains the internal organs in a disease-free condition.

As you build your physical center and powerhouse, you are simultaneously strengthening your emotional and spiritual center, your sense of self and your ability to nourish yourself with every thought and action you make. Practicing these asanas will enable you to create stability and consistency in your life and find the wherewithal to stay on course and not be knocked off center by extraneous people or events.

The way to begin is simple. Find a comfortable place to lie down on the floor, or if weather permits, to lie down on the ground outside. Position yourself face down with your legs straight out behind you and your arms and head in the most comfortable position that you can find. You may wish to add cushions under your chest or hips, or both, but aim to have your head and as much of your abdomen as possible against the ground.

All you need do now is to lie against the ground for a long time (this will be different for everyone, some people will find five minutes a long time, others will enjoy 20 minutes or so), remaining relaxed but alert. Begin by being aware of your breath, allowing yourself to breathe in through your nose and out through your mouth for at least a minute until you are relaxed enough to breathe effortlessly in through a wide bridged relaxed nose, letting the breath go smoothly and slowly.

Concentrate on your abdomen as it moves against the ground with your breath, making a conscious effort to sense the energy of the ground through your body, as you did through your feet or hands in earlier asanas. Aim to

Use the contact of the ground against your abdomen to renew your inner strength and resolve.

The affirmation for this asana is "The earth supports me."

establish a really good connection with the ground, releasing anxiety, tiredness, stress, and negativity into the ground on the exhalation, drawing nourishment and warmth from the ground into the center of your body as you breathe in. Move other parts of your body as you need to in order to be able to concentrate on the abdomen and remain completely at rest throughout the rest of your body.

Practicing this asana for increasing lengths of time will enable you to go deeper and deeper into this physical, emotional, and spiritual place of nourishment and calm that the Earth can give you, and will help you to build up your own reserves. It is a particularly useful asana to practice if you feel confused, disoriented, and worn out by the various onslaughts of your day.

*

Lie against the ground and inhale its sweet aroma as all negativity falls from you.

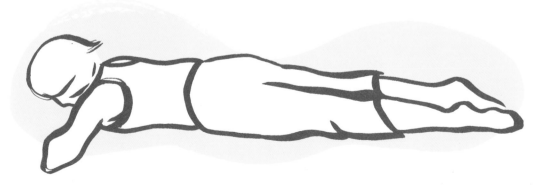

Cobra

The cobra holds the seat of wisdom in the center of its coiled form; it moves with its belly against the ground and its senses ever-watchful. To practice this asana you will need to have spent a couple of minutes in the previous asana preparing your body, mind, and breath.

1. pass from the first posture into the second stage, keeping your legs and hips passive and rooted to the ground, like a snake's, along their entire length. You may wish to gently rock your hips from side to side to release your spine.

2. lift the top of your torso by stretching your belly along the ground as though trying to make it move forward. Lift out of your front ribs and place your elbows on the floor to cradle your head in your hands. Remain here for some time until you are perfectly at ease with this shape. You may wish to lift your snake tail (your legs from the knee downward) and experiment with the sensations in your hips and abdomen and spine (aim to keep them passive throughout).

3. if you feel perfectly at peace with this posture you may wish to extend into the full posture. In order to do this, return to your original position lying flat against the ground, this time with the palms of your hands placed on the floor under your shoulders and your elbows tucked well in against the sides of your body. Your head should face directly forward with your chin against the ground.

4. take a few breaths to relax your legs and hips, and move your pubic bone down to push slightly against the ground. From this place, using the muscles of your abdomen and back (rather than just your shoulders and arms), deliberately extend your torso forward out of your pelvis, stretching the whole length of your abdomen and opening your chest as you rise forward and upward away from the floor. Your chin should move forward along the ground as your

*

The front and back of your body will extend if your hips and legs can open into the space of the ground.

The affirmation for this asana is "My own center is strong."

spine and abdomen extend, only lifting at the last moment to complete the journey with your neck opening at the front and back and your chin lifting.

5.   your spine will lengthen, your shoulders drop, and your neck extend. You may feel your abdomen stretching and opening right through your lower belly. Your back should feel free and open throughout.

Parighasana The Gate pose

This asana opens and trims the waist while strengthening and awakening the deep muscles of the lower belly from the pubic bone to the waist. It helps to awaken the energy that can sit dormant, or even stagnant, in the lowest parts of the body and psyche so that you can use it in a creative and positive way to nourish yourself and deepen your connection to all living things. It was also the asana that finally woke up my belly and returned it to me after the birth of each of my children; in other words, it helps to flatten your stomach after pregnancy and birth.

1. start by kneeling on a folded mat or blanket on a non-slip floor. Kneel so that your knees are hip width apart. Your knees, lower legs, and the tops of your feet should connect to the ground and become your anchors. At this point firmly tuck your pelvis under and keep it tucked in for the rest of the asana.

2. take a few breaths before putting one leg out to the side, turning out from the hip as you did for Trikonasana on page 82–3. If the sole of your foot does not make good contact with the ground, create a lift to support it, otherwise enjoy stretching the entire foot to the toes which should also be firmly against the ground.

3. having created your base, take your arms out to the side and rotate them at the shoulders so your palms face upward.

4.   when you are ready, exhale slowly, stretching first upward toward the sky and then to the top corner of the room, allowing the lower arm to slide along your leg and find a place to rest. The palm of your hand remains facing upward to remind you not to lean on the lower leg, but to use the muscles at the center of your body to support you. The top arm extends so that the side of your body can open from your hip through to your armpit. Avoid any feeling of collapse through the hips and keep your legs strong.

5.   use your inhalation to direct your attention to places in your body where you could release tension and soften, which you can consciously do as you exhale. Stay with the pose all the time you can keep it alive, growing and opening with your breath.

6.   to come out of the pose carefully travel back through the steps that you followed to arrive in the pose and rest, sitting back onto your feet before working with the other side. You will have quite a different experience working with the other side of your body, as with all asanas, so don't be afraid, for example, to use a lift for your foot on one side and not the other.

*

Your knee should turn upward in line with the top of your feet for this graceful asana.

Navasana

This asana is called the Boat pose because the shape that is created in some ways resembles a boat, but also because a degree of rocking backward and forward is involved in the early stages of its practice.

To be able to hold this asana for any length of time requires some strength through the length of the back and the abdomen. The wonderful thing about the way in which asana practice strengthens the abdomen in particular is that the muscles are elongated as they are built, creating a very lithe and graceful body that also has a remarkable degree of strength and stamina.

To begin this asana you will need to alert your sense of humor, bringing a smiling heart and face to the experience!

1. sitting on your mat with ample room around you, draw your knees toward your chest, drop your head, release the muscles of your jaw, and give your spine a good stretch. Release your head, extending your spine

The affirmation for this asana is "I am happy to be responsible for my life."

Enjoy the strength and fluidity of the center of your body, feeling your lower abdomen and back support your rising chi.

upward and feel the energy move up through your body from your hips.

2. stretch first one leg then the other to a diagonal position directed toward your extended arm and hand. Now that you have stretched your legs and alerted your body to the direction in which it is to be moving take a good breath in and as you exhale lift your arms and legs simultaneously.

3. once balanced in this position, concentrate on allowing the strength through your lower back and abdomen to develop—it definitely helps to have an awareness of chi flowing up through your body.

All the power of the asana comes from the lower body so avoid straining your upper back or shoulders or thrusting your neck forward in attempt to stay upright, because this will only compromise the whole pose and support the habit of avoiding having strength and power through the center. Sometimes people will maintain a healthy peripheral body, concentrating on upper body, arms, and legs while bypassing the center. This may be because activating the center involves waking up any emotions that have been held in that part of the body. Feeling powerless is often perceived as a state involving less responsibility than allowing all one's power to surface.

As one practices the asanas from this section of the book, it will become obvious that emotions of all sorts will start to surface. They do not necessarily need to be dealt with consciously, often the body will do all the work that is required if you are just willing to support it with attentiveness and your breath.

*

Have fun with this asana while you conjure its strength and beauty.

How our minds follow our bodies

Getting used to the feeling when emotions and all sorts of psychic, as well as physical, toxins that are stored in the body are released during and after asana practice is part of the advantage of practicing yoga in this very conscious and alert way. Nevertheless, it can be a little disconcerting for a novice who has not fully experienced the connection between body, mind, and soul before. It is one thing to acknowledge the connection, quite another to actually experience emotional release.

The best way to deal with this process is to stay very present, watching, as if in a film, the emotion lift out of the body and allowing time for the whole release to complete. This can involve a fair amount of humility as the full expression of the long repressed emotion surfaces and is spent. Continuing your asana practice beyond this point is important for any healing to be complete. Now that your practice has moved to a different level, you should work in even more respectful and attentive relation to your body.

Once you are able to incorporate this level of release and awareness into your practice it would be valuable to return to the midwinter/Water chi section of the book and revisit the asanas introduced here. Maybe you could set aside a time when you could work through the entire sequence slowly, carefully, and with a greater awareness of being able to empower your body using the four elements of chi that that we have looked at so far. This would add weight to your Earth chi practice. The addition of these new asanas that specifically address your center, your solar plexus, will increase the amount of chi that you can bring to all the asanas in the sequence.

As you return to each asana watch, or listen, or smell, or taste, the changes in your body. The more attentive that you become, the more information your body will give you and the more precise that information will become. The aim is to release toxicity of all kinds from your body as you practice, enabling your body to regenerate at a cellular level, having

*
The asanas will teach you to trust your body so that fears and trauma can be healed, allowing you to face your future with renewed vigor.

discarded residues of matter that are no longer useful, including memories, emotions, inherited beliefs, and a wide range of experiences.

In my early years as a healer I worked with a woman who released memories as we worked that her mother had passed to her. Significantly, it was practicing asanas that concentrated on her stomach and heart area together that produced the flood of images and huge emotional release, but I am convinced that it was only as part of a gradual and continuous release through her body that this was achieved.

Our bodies are very wise and will help us to heal at the deepest level if only we follow their lead.

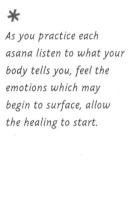

As you practice each asana listen to what your body tells you, feel the emotions which may begin to surface, allow the healing to start.

Emotional Wellbeing
An Overview

The range of emotional expression governed by Earth chi may appear broad, but as our understanding of the dynamics between the elements becomes more sophisticated (and therefore more useful), we can begin to appreciate the connections between apparently diverse qualities, such as those listed below:

- Dependency, codependency and the ability to be appropriately independent
- The ability to recognize the availability of a whole range of resources and use them well.

- The ability to nurture oneself and others in a balanced way.
- The confidence to access, mobilize, and act upon the full extent of one's personal power, physically, emotionally, and psychically.
- The insight to recognize the strength in vulnerability, passivity, humility, and service.
- The preparedness to give and receive love and support in equal measure.

These qualities are all an expression, in one way or another, of balanced Earth chi, which in itself is dependent on the degree of balance within, and between, all the other elements.

Look at the list above carefully and ask yourself where you stand in relation to these issues. If you find that you are unfamiliar with a few of them, see if you can appreciate the ways in which they might be connected. For example, the ability to nurture oneself and others in a balanced way is clearly related to a preparedness to give and receive. Perhaps you find one easy and not the other, or find yourself doing one and not the other. Why might that be? Is one half of the proposition more comfortable than the other? Perhaps it is easier to be in control, as you are when you are giving to, or nurturing, others. On the other hand, it might be frightening to be on the receiving end of love and support. Ask yourself why this might be. What exactly do you fear might happen if you allowed someone, or more than one person, to look after you for a while? You certainly would need to surrender control and focus on your own needs, possibly exposing some of them to yourself and the people around you.

There will be a payoff for anything that we experience as a sacrifice, whether it is always being the one giving out, or always being the victim who needs help. The payoff in the above scenario could be that, by focusing on others rather than yourself, you believe that you can retain a measure of control over your own vulnerability.

Hear the questions and hear your answers—inside you have the ability to love and be loved in equal measure. Enhancing your Earth chi will help you to listen to the needs of others, and to show your needs to those you love.

Connections

Connections between issues that sometimes seem disparate start to become more understandable if we look at the nature of Earth chi and then translate its qualities into an emotional expression. For example, if we have never

> In order to receive all the abundance that the Earth itself has to offer us, we need to be able to trust in the process of being taken care of in an unlimited and unconditional way.

✳

Trusting the Earth element to support you during the ebbs and flows of the yearly cycle requires you to learn how to accept the love and support with which you are surrounded. Only when you can begin to love yourself can you start to accept the support of the Earth chi.

experienced being cared for, or loved unconditionally, then it may be difficult to believe that we will be provided for, or that we can depend on others to play their part in our lives, so that we live in an interconnected way within a community of friends or family. If it is difficult to use the resources (in this case the people around us) that we have been given for this life, it may lead to a belief that we have to survive alone, without support or help from our environment, which we may even begin to think of as hostile.

How many people do you know that overtly or covertly subscribe to this world view, which in itself creates a way of behaving that actually promotes lack of support from their environment? In what ways do you share

> Look at the following statement and see how it resonates with you:
> "There may not be enough for me in the future."
> You may ask "enough of what?" and the answer would be "almost anything."

this world view? Many ways of behaving have this belief as their basis. This belief can sever the fundamental

Ask yourself the simple question "what may there not be enough of for me in the future?" and sit back and wait for the list to form.

connection to Earth chi and the great abundance that Earth supplies for every one of us.

A huge unraveling job can then begin. Do you recognize the way in which buying into this fundamental belief is separating you from the resources that are actually available to you, and which you are probably enjoying right now?

Earth as a Hostile Place

> "My survival and happiness depend on how other people judge my behavior."

When we are laboring under this belief daily life becomes a huge war zone in which we aim to gain approval for the things we do and avoid being found out for our inadequacies. We can never relax and simply know that whatever we do we will be loved and accepted. This belief, perversely, can lead us to behave in ways which are antisocial and detrimental to good relationships.

Left to our own devices and held within a caring community, most of us would be able to express our natural talents, live in a contented fashion, and make our contribution to the group. Consider, for a moment, that to be yourself, warts and all, is the very way to gain all the highest rewards society has to offer. Imagine all the barriers you have erected to protect yourself from others collapsing around you, and that the people you live among look at you with love, affection, and humor. Imagine them being delighted for you to be part of the group, welcoming the whole of you as a valuable, indispensable asset. Which parts of yourself, that in the past you had tried to conceal, suppress, or limit, would you most like to be valued as an asset?

In order to learn to accept yourself you must learn that others too will find you worthy. For some of us this sounds unobtainable, but take that first step—imagine how good this could be.

> Allow yourself to let go of your negative thoughts and connect with your inner Earth chi.

"I don't really trust that anything that I have been given is safe to use." This powerful belief will stop us from realizing our true potential, keep us

> By distancing ourselves from life's ongoing process we are distancing ourselves from the qualities that Earth chi offers.

starved of a whole range of available resources, and limit our involvement in life still further. It will also inhibit the development of our relationships with other people so that we starve ourselves on this level too. An intrinsic part of this belief is that some things are safe to use, but these are the things that other people have.

Ask yourself, "what are the things that life has given me that are not safe to use?" Looking at the list that you come up with may enable you to understand the ways in which you have chosen to distance yourself from life.

By distancing ourselves from life's ongoing process we are distancing ourselves from the qualities that Earth chi offers. We must allow ourselves to put roots deep down into the Earth, to connect with our own Earth chi which lies at the center of ourselves and who we are.

If we can reach out and echo that ability to connect to ourselves and our Earth in our relationships with others and the community as a whole, then we will be healing any imbalance in our own Earth chi and the role it plays as one of the five transforming elements which make up the whole.

*

The joy and freedom of children is ours. Listen to your heart—in the silence of your soul you still hold that joy. Living in tune with the Earth chi will allow you to tap into your inner strength.

Earth as a friendly place

If we are able to bring ourselves to believe that the Earth is essentially a friendly place, and our experience of receiving Earth chi is a positive one, how would this belief affect our feelings and behavior? If we no longer need to defend ourselves against the ever-present threat of actually fully participating in life, or losing our control, then just imagine what might happen—our relationship with life might improve greatly.

It's good to know that there are things that can be done to increase our chances of feeling this way and experiencing life more fully. We all know people by whom we felt totally accepted, with whom we feel completely at ease. What happens to us when we are in their company? We may behave in ways that reflect who we really are. We may do things that are more about expressing who we are and less conditioned by the people around us. We may exhibit a wider range of feelings, beliefs, and behavior. We might experiment more by expressing new or developing parts of ourselves. We may stick less rigidly to stereotypical or expected ways of behaving. These liberating ways of behaving will help us to access our own power, build our sense of self and our inner strength. Ultimately, we will feel supported, nurtured, inspired, and keen to participate in life more actively and fully.

This is the opposite of coming away from a group of people feeling tired, low spirited, and in some way smaller and less able to continue your day in a positive, constructive, and alert way. Once it is easy to identify the difference between the two experiences it is possible to actively seek out the people who make you feel more alive and avoid, or let go of, those who deaden your chi.

> If you surround yourself with damaged people who relate with the Earth as a hostile place, then it is harder to experience life as a friendly supportive process yourself. Why not support yourself by spending time with people, and in places and situations, that make you feel more alive, and more confident to feel that way?

*

Learning to accept yourself for who you are will draw others to you, to bask in your glow of confidence, so you too become a healing influence on all those around you.

One of the first questions my spiritual teacher ever asked me was "What are the things in your life that nurture you?" He followed this by asking "What are the things in life that no longer nurture you?" The responses to these two questions can form the kingpin of a whole way of being and acting that will support you in being the person you really are, putting you in a position to receive Earth chi in such a way that everything else in your life becomes part of a usable whole.

Food
Different foods for different times

Different days and times require different types and different amounts of food. From the small snack to the huge feast, all meal types are necessary to keep you healthy and vigorous.

Why should the same foods eaten at different times do different things for us? We have already looked at the reasons why foods eaten in different contexts will feed us in different ways; we can now add time to the food equation. Looking at the world as an energetic place that we are very much a part of involves acknowledging the roles that both time and space play in the creation and development of our own chi. It makes sense, therefore, to take on board the idea that we need to eat differently at different times in our lives, or just during the day.

Everyone accepts that babies need to eat differently from adults. Some people recognize that children as a whole need to eat differently from adults (I don't just mean the strange "let's make life easy for ourselves" idea that they need more packaged junk food). But how many people have considered the massive difference in nutritional dynamics between a young adult going through puberty and an elderly person? Why shouldn't food support you specifically for the part of your life that you are engaged in? How ludicrous to complain that no sooner has your teenage son finished dinner than he is back in the kitchen eating a snack!

Why should you be surprised when your girlfriend, who is in the middle of her menstrual cycle, doesn't want to stop for lunch at all, and when she (two days before the onset of her period) wants to eat every two hours? I was amazed (and relieved) to learn recently that women need 800 calories a day more in the days preceding each menstrual period, and that the heightened appeal of food at this time is perfectly natural and actually supports the body in its process. Why isn't this essential information more widely known?

If you can accept that you need different foods and ways of cooking, serving, and eating at different times of the day, and of the year, then it makes sense to eat differently at different times in your own body cycles. These may not just be the big life-changing times, but within each of these cycles others will be turning, and within these still more. It is a complete denial of the purpose of food to attempt to impose a similar way of eating on yourself day in and day out. To use available resources in a way that nourishes you as an individual living within a group necessitates thinking more about differing needs, not only between people, but for each person over time.

Growing flexibility around food

There is a well-documented trend among large groups of the population, particularly in Europe and the U.S., away from eating large well-spaced meals, and toward a more continuous grazing approach. This may have something to do with people eating less meat and high animal-content food, or it may be connected with changing social and economic patterns. Either way, why not be positive about it and see it as an opportunity to try a different way of being around food?

Since most of us have an abundance of food available to us (obesity is now officially more of a concern worldwide than malnutrition), we can enjoy the luxury of having a more fluid approach to the business of food and meals. In the past, a lot of the rigidity around the creation, serving, and eating of food was based on the strictures of a limited food supply. Now we have the luxury to do it differently, so let's enjoy that resource.

Most people's desire to keep to existing styles of cooking and eating meals seems to be based on the fear that they may lose out on some of the social and ritualistic elements of eating. Why might this be so? If the food that is cooked to be eaten together has been reduced to a prepackaged meal microwaved and eaten infront of the TV, then what is

lost in its passing? Anyone involved in such a souless event will have little investment in hanging on to it. Similarly, anyone who is reduced to perpetually eating a solitary dinner after working a 14-hour day must feel free to move to new ways of approaching food.

At the other end of the spectrum, food cooked, and eaten, communally can still be the single most important exchange within a group and is something to cherish, but anyone participating regularly, or at all, in that type of event has no reason to let that go, and won't. People may have stopped cooking and eating in the traditionally acceptable fashion, but food culture and ceremonial styles of eating together are far from dead.

I suggest that we stop feeling guilty about the ways in which we choose to enjoy food and look at the really positive things that can be gained from a more flexible approach. This can only support us in that it is more in tune with our bodies' needs and return us to a position of anxiety- and guilt-free eating. Imbalances in Earth chi are usually easily identifiable as problems—real or imagined— around eating such as weight problems, difficulty cooking for, or eating in the company of, others, problems with stockpiling food, or obsessing over certain types of food. Alternatively, or often additionally, we develop food allergies, and inabilities to adequately digest, as well as compulsive dependence on,

and obsessive concern about, all sorts of foods.

Anything that we can do to help us make friends with food again has got to be to everyone's advantage.

When it comes to eating listen to your body—it knows how much it should have, what it should eat, and when. Trust yourself and you can't really go wrong.

Making friends with food

What can we do to make friends with food again? To start with, we could aim to become good friends in a mutually supportive relationship, one in which we are not obsessive, but maintain other satisfying, stimulating and rewarding interests. We could become the sort of friend happy to renegotiate the habitual pattern of the relationship as circumstances change, ready to accommodate and even welcome that change.

If food has become something that is absolutely central to your life and which you spend a considerable time thinking about, maybe you could consider broadening your food-based activity to include something related to, but not entirely concentrated on, food. If you are going to eat a huge tub of ice cream, why not go to the movies and eat a slightly smaller one while you watch a film? If you have started a new diet, why not involve a friend and make it something you discuss together—you may even get to talk about some other things as well! If you find it difficult to eat when you are stressed, why not get into a routine of preparing your food half an hour before you plan to eat it and spend that time doing something that will promote your relaxation and nurture you, reminding yourself how it feels to look after yourself.

*

Food should be important in your life, but not so important that you become obsessed either with eating or not eating.

Another thing that you can do to renegotiate your relationship to food is to make everything to do with eating different from usual. For example, buy your food in a different place, use completely different ingredients when you put a meal together, and cook familiar food in a totally new way. You could alter the habitual pattern of your time of eating. If you usually shower and dress before breakfast, reverse the order. Or if you eat one large meal as soon as you get home, try two small snacks instead. You will be changing the messages that you give to yourself about how food and the experience of eating has to be for you.

You could also change the place in which you eat and the utensils that you use. Try changing from all white crockery to all orange, or from one large plate for everything to three small bowls, one for each type of food. If you usually eat alone, eat one meal in three in company, or vice versa.

All of these thing will completely realign your relationship with food. You will be taking your power back, calling the shots and moving out of victim mode. It feels great, is hugely liberating, and will reveal to you a lot about your relationship to food and the way in which you are prepared to nourish yourself.

Changing your eating routine will show you options that you have never considered and open you up to new possibilities.

5

Fall/Metal

· ·

Introduction

Once the great display and activity of the Fire season has moved through the transforming space of Earth, all outward display of passion is turned toward its center once again. Fall arrives, and Metal chi is expressed through every place and moment. The chi of the planet directs all momentum back downward and inward. Before it can reach the fullest moments of yin and midwinter/Water energy, the chi must first take due time to gather in and focus, just as in nature the great summer crop is harvested and brought in for use in condensed form as grain and fruit and seed. So at this time we also reap the rewards, or just desserts, of the thinking, planning, and acting phases of our own cycle.

At this time, Metal chi accumulates, moving back toward its source, the Earth.

In the process it is contracting, solidifying, taking on mass, and evolving toward structure. Think of the role of metal in your life, its qualities, and the contribution it makes. Visualize the copper pipes that carry water and the cables and circuits that facilitate the movement of energy. Think for a moment of the steel that lies within the concrete structures that contain and support your day-to-day living.

This bright hot intense energy is the accumulated product of chi, raining down from the great breadth of the heavens, the physical and etheric structures that lie beyond the limits of our own planetary sphere. This immense downpouring, which meets the turbulent and irregular upward movement erupting erratically from the horizontal outward movement of Fire chi, is mediated by the centralizing impetus of Earth chi, whose role is to turn this heavenly chi into manifest resources. So the myriad layers of color, texture, light, and abundance that were the essence of late summer pass into the golden glow of the setting sun, as the bundles of fruits and grains are gathered ready to be transported to a place of winter storage. Early evening brings people home from work, families and friends gather, light turns from gold to dusk, and twilight brings the world alive in quite a different and altogether more melancholic and otherworldly way.

The mystery of this chi, this season and time of day, is like the alchemist's work, which transforms base metals into precious gold. So we can say that within each of us the alchemist is at work as we allow our own chi

The myriad layers of color, texture, light, and abundance that were the essence of late summer pass into the golden glow of the setting sun, as the bundles of fruits and grains are gathered ready to be transported to a place of winter storage.

*

Fall at its best is twilight in its most essential form—a really satisfying deep breath that inspires and enlivens on the inhalation, nourishes at its moment of pause, and satisfies and fills one with joy on its release. So in working to balance Metal Chi it is time to seek out your angels, learn how to breathe, and watch your harvest rolling in.

to open and receive the abundance of Earth chi. Through our ability to allow that chi to suffuse through our bodies, releasing the chaff from the grain as it goes, we are gathering with each moment the essence, or the seed, that can be held by ourselves through a time of contemplation and rest, ready to be used for each of our new beginnings. So with our understanding of the nature and role of Metal, we complete our understanding of the cycle that we are part of and that is us.

In Chinese medicine, the lungs and large intestine are seen as the organs that govern Metal chi. These functioning systems control respiration and elimination respectively. Broadly speaking, respiration enables us to use Heaven's energy, or chi, in our physical body, while the large intestine gathers everything that we don't need and lets it go. By expelling as waste that part of the gathered chi (whether it be air or food) that will not nurture us, we become microcosms of the universal cycle of growth.

In Chinese thought, it is the ability to accept the breath down into the body (to accept the descending chi as it rains down), that is the key to the balanced functioning of this part of the elemental cycle. As such, the ability to breathe well through a whole range of situations is seen as the key to vibrant physical health, just as the ability to accept the chi that is a reflection of the magnitude of its source, is the key to the spiritual and emotional part of the bargain.

Thus our ability to feel our position, who we are, and what we can contribute, is measured by this ability to allow chi to flow though us as it meets Earth from Heaven. While the attainment of balanced Earth Chi is dependent on the ability to allow the being to become suffused by yin, finding balanced Metal chi may be said to have a lot to do with the ability to supply a channel for yang.

Indicators of balanced Metal chi may equally be the ability to organize, consolidate, and communicate, to be physically energetic or even athletic, to have a home that is clutter-free, well structured, and stylish and, in addition, the ability to enjoy a heightened intuitive—even clairvoyant—ability.

Feng Shui
The Shaman's house

In this house the Shaman pulls the worlds into one—one place, one flow, one rhythm. The essential is lifted down through the swirling layers of human paraphernalia and condensed into a structure both clear and pure in its intensity. Light pours in through windows and is led around the rooms and hallways, bouncing off walls and floors, threading its way down glinting metal ornamentation and broad sweeps of color. Heaven comes to Earth and arrives as structure—clear, bright, and shining.

Slate, granite, stone and marble structures become focal. Color is condensed and washed through with translucent white and silver, manifesting itself in fabrics, which diffuse light into dappled patterns. Floors are swept bare, except for a flock of rugs that only just settle on the ground, and are ready at any moment to take flight and reappear as wall hangings.

A space that expresses a preponderance of Metal chi is minimalist, with streaks of lightning-inspired artwork, and more solid shapes of hewn rock and dense wood. Neither good nor bad, in itself this type of space has more to do with alchemy than comfortable living or nurturing the physical body. It will feed the spirit and enliven the soul, but—at its most extreme—its

Metal chi is light and shiny, comfort is brought through soft fabrics. It is light and airy, white and wood, but it needs tempering with the warmth of Earth and the Fire of summer.

energy may just drift off into the ether, or, more likely, contract and condense into a tight, inextricable knot.

If you recognize elements of your space in this description, then that indicates that you have a healthy relationship with this quality of chi. If, however, you are looking around the very space that has just been described—except that you have less color, no fabrics, and have replaced your wooden floors with concrete—then you may want to ask yourself "what next?" and 'where do I go from here?" The ability to create structure and unity, and to extract beauty out of function, along with the compulsion to go on and on reducing everything to one perfect line can be somewhat addictive. Just as that perfect piece of greenery edged with just a suggestion of orange peel may be an absolute delight to the senses but won't feed your body, so a bedroom full of white linen and bleached wood will not hold you safe enough to sleep and dream until morning.

We all have something of the Shaman within us, and are all capable of feeling some element of the holiness of simplicity distilled from complexity. We can all appreciate the transforming power of a stormy sky or the smell of the ground after the rain has fallen, but homes are for living in as human beings with human needs. We need to take the best of the Shaman's house and feed it with the resourceful nurturing Earth, absorbing those deep midwinter layers, nooks, and crannies, invigorating and lifting it with spring spirit, and letting it blaze with the passion of Fire.

Fluid Structures

Achieving a balance of the elements in a house is one of the most challenging aspects of practicing Feng Shui. Each space should express a different balance according to the time of year, the needs of the people living there, and the particular ways in which they need supporting. Of course, all of these requirements are constantly shifting and changing, and the whole dynamic of the group, as well as each lone individual, changes with them. Having animals living alongside us adds to the mix of needs and aspirations.

It is for this reason that I often look at some interior design and some building practices and wonder if the designers wish us all to lead static lives, fixed in one moment of time, the moment when the last tile or brick, or cushion or vase was placed. What will happen next month, or next week when it needs to change?

This is where balanced Metal chi saves the day by helping us to provide ourselves with structures that are functional, solid, and exist to facilitate movement and change. Think about it—if the need to move things around, change light levels, add or remove layers, was built into design concepts, wouldn't that be a huge step toward allowing people to grow and change and respond effortlessly to changes in their lives? The ability to adapt to change is one of the major

Each season and each person requires something different from a home. Your house should adapt to the changes from the heat of summer to the frost of winter, and to the natural flow of your life.

keys to being able to achieve and maintain good health. Space that is designed to allow for changing needs for privacy, or needs to be more or less active and creative, or desires to spend more or less time socializing, or even just the tendency to be warm and cozy in the winter and expansive and active in the summer, are therefore health-supporting.

Consider, for a moment, your own space. How versatile is it, or how built-in, fixed, and immovable? Do you have whole groups of things that, in your opinion, simply can't be moved—be they a shelf of coffee pots or a wall of shelves? How much of the structure of your home do you see as absolutely immovable? Could you move doorways, walls, floors, or even the staircase if you decided that it would better serve your purpose? How would it make you feel to change the front door to another location entirely? Have you chosen a space where almost no structural change, or no change at all is possible?

As always, it is about getting the balance right. Clearly, living in a space where walls and doors are moved annually or even more often would be ludicrous, but how many of our ancestors were nomads, living without any structures? Maybe other things can provide structure in our lives and we can lose a little of the rigidity that may have evolved around the physical structures, and here I include objects, in our space. The desire to create structure for ourselves is frequently identified with stability, but maybe it is no more than false attachment, and it is distancing us from more vital and living connections to the world around us.

Maybe other things can provide structure in our lives and we can lose a little of the rigidity that may have evolved around the physical structures in our space.

Houses not Prisons

If we are in the business of creating homes not tombs, then we can blow away the cobwebs of "should" and "ought" to create living, breathing spaces that support, not contain, protect, not imprison, liberate, not restrict. You do not need to find a place for any item, style, or design that you feel you "ought" to have. Ask yourself the following questions:

You are not confined by your home, you can, in fact, be liberated by it; the options it offers are the options of lifestyle.

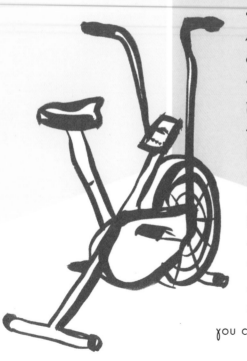

- How many dining rooms do people actually dine happily in?

- How many living rooms have become places to impress, rather than places of ease and wonder?

- How many unwanted gifts clutter up spaces, suffocating the spirit around them and deadening the growing chi?

- Do you give space to an exercise bike because you feel you shouldn't be fat? Why not give the space to a double hammock or a bed for the puppy you always wanted instead?

- Do you paint your walls beige because you feel you don't deserve cerise, or upholster your chairs in burgundy when you long to be surrounded by cream?

- Have your built-in kitchen and your built-in bedroom and your built-in study just ended up building you into a corner, where you feel you can't even think straight?

Creating a home that does not simply follow rules will allow you to do the same. Your life is so much more. Define it by who you are, not by the space you live in.

What are you aiming to protect and guard in these fortresses? And what would happen if you dismantled them, just a little, and allowed them to breathe more freely? Maybe your structure, stability, and focus would be allowed to develop on other levels. Your power base could shift so that it was focused on your internal being, instead of being based on things that are external to you. Then it could suffuse the way you behave and think and feel, enabling you to experience life, more directly, through your senses. By cultivating the ability to live in a more immediate way, without mediating every experience through some physical structure or object, you will find the way to a more direct relationship with the solidity and structure that is an expression of your connection to yang chi. If you let it, it will create a strength for you that is of a totally different nature to the strength you seek from the acquisition of seemingly immovable objects.

The structures that you create in your spaces could actually facilitate your connection to the living vibrant world around you, supporting your intention to learn to be more fully conscious, more widely awake. But you can only approach that position by developing an awareness of the energetics of your physical world. So we return to the Shaman's house, where it is recognized that a chair is not a chair, but a bundle of sensory messages, vibrations, and images around which we are building our world, whether we choose to accept it or not.

Houses fit for Angels

Once you have looked at the land around the house where you live, and traced a boundary line between your space and the space beyond it, it is time to look at the quality of chi in your space. Does it feel clear and focused and alive? Is the chi so clear that a rainbow of light and color washes the space from top to bottom? Land and buildings have auras, just as we do—energy fields that can shine bright and full spectrum, sitting in arcs that extend far beyond the reaches of the physical space. Like us, if a piece of land or a building enjoys balanced chi, and attracts love, support, and nurturing, it will reflect that physical quality and attract more of the same. But sometimes a space has been damaged, and has a ragged, dull aura that seems to be unable to rebalance and assert its natural beauty and wisdom. Then people living on that land, in that space may find that they too are experiencing difficulties, particularly in connecting to Heaven's energy, the vital yang chi that supports their Metal chi, and completes their own personal circle.

The homes that we live in both reflect us and form us. The chi within us is reflected by our personal space.

Manifestations of depleted Metal chi include difficulties in completing tasks, closing deals (or being paid for work done), things promised and not delivered, problems with authority, responsibility, and commitment, difficulties in managing and organizing, and breakdowns in communication. The physical symptoms might manifest as asthma, eczema, chronic fatigue syndrome, other immune deficiency illnesses, irritable bowel syndrome, allergies, or the inability to father a child. The body, mind, and spirit need to be able to participate in the exchange that fosters Metal chi. Feng Shui remedies that address the land that a building sits on, as well as the energetic circumstances of a building, are often needed to enable Metal chi to harmonize and complete the elemental cycle.

You can do much to assist a space in rebalancing itself by following the simple Feng Shui laid out in this book, and in *Feng Shui In Ten Simple Lessons*, but it may prove more of a challenge if you live on a piece of land that is under prolonged attack from something linked to past use. This may simply be physical abuse, as when a space has been used for dumping waste, or carrying physical structures such as pipelines. Or maybe the space

If your space remains dim and gloomy, despite all your efforts then it's likely that the site needs extra help for it to heal. When you walk around your home listen to your heart and you will know if all is not well.

has suffered from psychic contamination, possibly because it was the site of great suffering or difficulty. Disturbances in the land, or dishonorable building practices, or simply appalling Feng Shui in the design of a building, can be enough to interfere with a space's integrity in such a way as to impair its ability to transmute yang chi, thus keeping its Metal chi in a permanently depleted condition.

Remedying a Space's Aura

Just like you, your space deserves to be allowed to function at its best, to be filled with positive energy. If your home still feels off-key after clearing then it's time to call in an expert.

All spaces, all land, deserve to be loved and healed. To simply notice that the space does, in fact, have life is a sure way to remedy Metal imbalance and set healing in motion. A space has intention, purpose, beauty, and grace, but sometimes these things haven't been acknowledged for a long time. All too often, a space is just about hanging on in there, pulling down enough chi to keep Metal doing its job, and supporting us just enough for the difficulties to go unnoticed. Land that has been damaged, and is still damaged, needs healing either on a physical level, (by changing Feng Shui to allow chi to flow through in a supportive and nurturing way, or by changing, or removing, physical structures to enable the land to heal), or on an etheric level. You may be able to do this yourself by continuous, purposeful, and well intentioned work directed toward clearing the space up and making it healthy and whole again, or you may need to call in an expert. This would be a healer with experience working with damaged land or buildings, a Shaman, a priest, or a group of people with enough knowledge and experience of healing generally to be able to facilitate the return to health of the land and building.

Very often, witnessing a problem and the intention to heal it is all that is needed to return a space to good health and get that chi flowing again. Then the whole rainbow of colors in the aura can shine again, and the structure of the space can resonate clearly and freely. Everyone using the space will experience a feeling of clarity and increased vitality, plants and trees will thrive more readily, and life will regain its natural flow and harmonious order. If Metal is out of balance there can be no alchemy, no transformation from earthly matter into life and light. Life becomes dull, meaningless, and little more than a struggle to survive day to day.

Here is a simple visualization that will help support the Metal chi of your space. You can do it once, or for a few days at dusk until you feel that the job is completed.

First allow yourself to become conscious of your own breathing and the way that you have settled yourself against the ground. Wait until you can breathe even more freely and feel that you can rest against the ground with more complete trust in having the time and space to complete this healing visualization. Timing is important, so have the patience to wait for the right moment to begin.

When you are ready, simply imagine the land that your home is built on, look in your mind's eye deep down into the Earth and then reach up into the building continuing your inward gaze up into the sky. Notice any places where there seems to be a disconnection, a break in the rhythm or flow of your gaze. Simply hold your attention at those places, focusing on an intention to heal and reconnect each part with all the others, and with the full spectrum from Earth to Heaven and back again to the deepest place in the Earth. Use your inhalation to hold your attention and your exhalation to move your attention and when you have finished take a few cycles of breath to clear and strengthen your own chi.

Yoga
The Breath of Life

The first asana in this section directs your attention to your breath. Begin by choosing a way to sit so that you are both symmetrically positioned and comfortable. It can help to sit on a thick folded blanket of red and orange. Spend some time sitting quietly, paying absolute attention to the rhythm and quality of your breathing. Begin by allowing each breath to drop deep down into your body as you inhale. You will need to relax your belly and hips, feeling your hips become wide and open and your stomach soften and expand downward and outward. As your spine lifts up to carry your torso high and expand the space of your abdomen, your side ribs and back ribs can expand with your breath. Allow your back to feel warm and expansive. You can practice this asana with a wide sash of cloth tied around your middle and lower back. Choose a cloth in a rich warm color (gold is an obvious choice), avoiding white or blue.

At the top of each breath allow a sensation of the breath rising up through the body to warm your heart and fill the back of your throat. As you continue to sit and breathe, allow the back of your neck to lengthen and your jaw to soften, feeling the bridge of your nose widening and the entire nasal cavity softening. The skin around your nose and extending up between your eyebrows may tingle with the breath and feel as though it is stretching and waking up. As you allow each inhalation to drop deep into your body and fill it, then rise high up though your abdomen, neck, and head, you may find that eventually you reach a moment of pause at the end of your inhalation. At this moment of pause allow stillness and peace to diffuse your body and imagine the bones of your skull sliding apart to allow the top of your head to open so that the breath rises to a place beyond the limits of your physical body. Allow this time to last as long as the breath is held without struggle or effort, it may only be a split second, before allowing the breath to leave your body entirely without reservation or fear.

Find a balanced way to sit in which you can really relax your hips and legs and lengthen your spine. Then your head will balance perfectly and your breath can flow.

Imagine allowing your body to be absolutely still without holding onto breath (or life) in every part and cell of its being, and allow the space and time to be at peace as all the breath drains away down into the ground on which you are sitting. Having the faith to let go of your breath and attachment to life in every fiber of your being is the key to arriving at a place of enlightenment and tranquillity, located at the moment of stillness before the desire to reconnect and participate in life is renewed in the form of the slow beginning of the desire to breathe in again.

Seated Twist

I would recommend always beginning practice with the grounding method of breathing, which includes breathing in though the nose and out through the mouth, and incorporating the breath of life asana discussed on the previous page once you are at ease with yourself as your session progresses. The breath in yoga acts as a bridge between body and mind. It is particularly important to pay careful attention to the breath when practicing the asanas in this section of the book, which is after all about balancing Metal chi. Lung function and the ability to receive Heaven's energy and to let go of waste are the keys to this element.

    The seated twist illustrated on this page is an example of an asana that works to free the spine and strengthen its entire length. Rotating the spine is an often neglected but essential part of maintaining its strength and flexibility, and therefore of its overall good health.

            To arrive in this asana follow the stages as illustrated,

*
Gathering your limbs into your body will focus your energy so that your spine can unfold and revitalize your whole being.

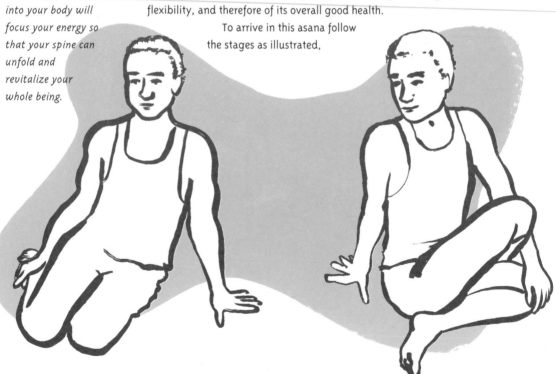

The affirmation for this asana is "There is no separation in my body, only ease of connection."

The more you lengthen your spine, the more freedom you have to rotate from the base.

allowing your hips and legs to form the base of the posture. Right from the beginning, when you are seated with your legs folded to the side, keep your spine long and avoid any feeling of collapse or compression. When you bring one leg over the other allow your hips and legs to open and relax as much as possible before you proceed. You could choose to support your hips with a cushion if this helps you to secure a solid easy base. The rotation of the spine will feel like a spiraling upward, and will move more freely and easily if you work with your breath to support and reassure your body.

You will be able to move into this posture more and more easily as you increase the strength of each part of your spine by working each section and lifting upward strongly. Elongating the spine and encouraging each part of it to strengthen and rotate in equal measure is the key to success. Be aware of the position of your neck and head as the point of release for the spiraling energy that is flowing from the base of your spine, and visualize its continuing journey into the ether. Likewise, be aware of the root that lies at the beginning of that spiral, way beyond the base of your body. As your base becomes more open and stronger the amount of energy that your body will be able to take in and channel will increase.

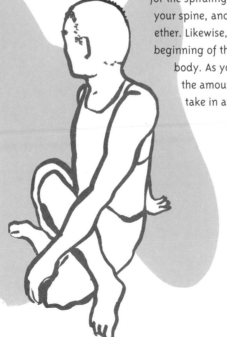

Circular Breathing

This is a fantastic asana for enhancing the breath and encouraging completion in our bodies and lives.

1. begin with your feet together against the ground, as one foot. Visualize one strong root descending into the ground and allow your breath to move freely through your body down into the ground at this one point. Lift both arms to stretch high above your head so that the backs of your hands come together to make one hand.

2. release your shoulders and let go of all attempts to push your arms up to the sky with the effort of your upper back and shoulders. Visualize strong supple wings lifting out of two places alongside the center of your back in two great arcs. Keep the back of your neck long and allow your masks to drop from your face. Some people have found it helpful to name each mask they wish to release—for example, the

*

Let your eyes close and feel the circle unfold around you with your movement and breath.

mask you wear as an employee, as a mother or father, as a neighbor, as a friend, as a householder, and so on.

3. now begin to move toward the ground with the exhalation, allowing one side of your body to open as the other side performs the balancing role of resting and releasing. Take the whole length of your exhalation to arrive at a position with one arm resting along your leg and the other arm lifting still, skyward. You may lift your head to look up at the moment of pause in your breath if you feel this helps to express the asana more fully.

4. as you begin to inhale, follow your breath with your movement, lifting your body back to a central position, taking the whole length of your inhalation to arrive at the top with the backs of your hands together again. Rest during the pause, before the next exhalation sees you traveling downward—this time to the other side. Again, one side of the body gives way as one side opens, just as the exhalation makes way for the inhalation.

This movement with the breath can continue, always following the breath rather than allowing the movement of the body to impose the rhythm of breath. Be aware of the sides of the ribs opening and becoming mobile, and the sides of the waist and hips opening as well. The neck should feel free and easy, and an increased awareness of the sides of the neck and head, including the ears and inner ears will reward anyone who has enough patience to stay with this asana for a few breaths after they feel they have "done enough."

Squat

I first came across this variation of the classical squat, with feet closer together, when I was pregnant with my first child and began to learn prenatal yoga. I have been using it with men, women, and children ever since to huge advantage, and practice it myself whenever I lose sight of the fact that my body and mind are one, and that where there is an outside there is an equally important inside.

This asana opens the hips, strengthens the legs and back, and invigorates the pelvic floor. It also focuses the mind wonderfully and brings you down to earth with its recreation of such a wonderfully solid and squat shape.

As with all asanas, the shapes you make are sacred geometry in action, and as you move into this position you will see how sometimes you need first to go low in order to be able to fly high. The movement within stillness, the dynamic that creates the balance between the opposing forces, is epitomized by this asana, which becomes an expression of Metal chi in balance.

There is no precise, or even elegant, way to arrive in this asana, although I would say that however you get there is part of the pose and should be treated as such. Aim to keep your heels on the ground, if need be tuck a folded rug under your heels. Your feet should be placed wide enough to let your body move through the space between your knees

1. allow your hips to sink to the ground, your belly to first relax and then lift with your back, upward out of your hips and legs. Pay careful attention to what you are doing with your mouth and jaw; try to keep them relaxed and fluid. Your feet should be well anchored to the ground at all four corners and feel alive and strong, with your ankles lifting strongly upward.

2. release your shoulders and allow your arms to support the backward motion of your legs as your body moves through the wide space of your open pelvis. Your chest should feel open and not in any way cramped. All your internal organs should feel supported and expansive, with your breathing clear and strong.

*

If you need to put a folded rug underneath your heels, do so and let your legs rest while your feet and ankles are strong and grounded.

With this asana you have come down to meet the ground and changed your shape to accommodate the inside of your physical body, which is supported and given security by the outside. It encourages a new awareness of how the outside and inside work together to create a whole, the one moving to accommodate the other. The palms of the hands come together to add strength to the upper part of the structure and perfectly express the unity of the whole.

The affirmation for this asana is "All things are one."

Ustrasana
The Camel

This is a very strong back bend and is really invigorating. Practice this asana when your energy is low and you will feel your chi level rising.

I like to practice this posture against a wall, as proximity to the wall helps to keep the body lifted into the correct alignment. The classical version of this posture instructs us to begin with feet and knees together, but a greater amount of freedom can be enjoyed if you practice the asana with knees and feet positioned hip width apart.

Begin by kneeling facing a wall with a thick nonslip rug under your legs and feet. The tops of your feet should be resting along the ground, with the lower part of your legs and the tops of your feet creating a good connection with the ground. Your knees should be in contact with the wall.

It is very important to tuck your hips well under and keep them in this position for the length of your journey in and out of this asana. The aim is to open your body and enhance its strength, with your lower back feeling long and supported throughout. Strength through your legs, abdomen, hips, and the whole length of your back should cooperate to allow your body to open into this movement. Your lower back should not feel squeezed or restricted at any time.

1. place your hands on your hips, and while keeping the lower part of your body stationary, open your upper chest and allow your neck to open and your head to fall back. Enjoy a series of deep breaths, paying particular attention to your inhalation.

2. relax your throat and forehead and keep your arms and elbows moving toward each other behind your back with your shoulders moving down. You may feel the front of your thighs beginning to stretch and open, but aim to keep your thighs as close to the wall as possible.

3. after some breaths return to an upright position and regain a feeling of calm and balance. If you found this part of the asana easy, you may wish to continue to the next stage.

As your thighs and hips move forward to meet the wall, your legs and feet act as a balancing tail. Then your upper body can open and give voice.

*

Allow your throat to open as the top of your chest expands and your whole neck softens.

4. proceed as above, but this time move into a position with your hands connecting to your heels or ankles. Arrive in this position one hand at a time, working carefully until your body feels ready to move into the full posture.

5. once there, concentrate on using your inhalation to encourage your back to expand and your thighs to gain strength, and your exhalation to allow your whole body to soften and release in a motion that travels up from your legs, through your hips and torso, over your neck and face, and back toward the ground. Visualizing this arc as a full rainbow of colors helps the asana to find its own rhythm and flow.

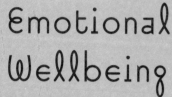

Emotional Wellbeing

The connection between the emotional and the physical

The ability to assimilate heavenly chi through the breath forms the foundation for creating balanced Metal chi. The respiratory system is perceived to control one's awareness of the physical world, not only through the sensory organ the nose, (which contributes so much to our sense of taste as well as smell), but also because of the direct connection between the lungs and skin (whose role in respiration is fully acknowledged). Metal chi is therefore directly connected to the ability to absorb and assimilate all vibrational life in our surroundings. The large intestine (partner to the lungs in this analysis), as the organ of elimination, is responsible for supporting our ability to discard material which is no longer relevant or has become obsolete.

Thus, to enjoy strong Metal chi is to be intensely sensitive to your environment, be it physical, emotional, or spiritual. To be able to focus on that which is essential or useful for your current state and hold onto it, until what you need has been distilled from the whole, and the surplus is released back into

the environment, much as stale air or waste matter is released. The combination of this ability to absorb, assimilate, and eliminate is the key to maintaining balanced Metal chi.

The ability to absorb information from the environment is dependent on your ability to be alert or conscious, alive in your very being, rather than slightly desensitized or numb, a state you may become habitually dependent on creating for yourself. It is reasonable that at times of perceived threat you might find ways to deaden your senses in order to protect yourself from emotional pain, real or anticipated. Most of us have become expert at devising ways to "dodge" oncoming feelings, be they simple devices like drinking or eating foods to desensitize ourselves and make us feel more passive and less alert, or the more sophisticated tendency to manipulate our environment so as to create comfort zones for ourselves, unfortunately at the expense of blocking out whole sections of reality. Pain is increasingly seen as something to be avoided rather than as something that should be embraced as part of an early warning system signaling to us that something is wrong and needs attention.

In order to support your chi you could consider rethinking your approach to the vibrational world around you, building your inner strength so that you are able to receive a wide range of stimuli without fear of being knocked off balance. In this way, you will be able to open your senses to a wider range of information that will support you in your own personal journey, in the simple business of day-to-day living.

The more breath you can take in, the more you can fuel your body, the more fully you need to exhale so that you can begin the process again. Similarly with your emotional life, the more you can allow in, the more richness there is to absorb, assimilate, and express. But this whole process is of course also dependent on your ability to let go of everything that is no longer useful.

Focusing and enhancing your Metal chi will increase your ability to absorb the chi around you—the benefits will go beyond Metal to encompass all the elements.

Developing Intuition and the Ability to Let Go

A person with well balanced Metal chi enjoys a powerful ability to use information from the outside world. They may even be seen to have some mystical ability or additional source of information not available to other people. These people have quite simply a more developed sense of the vibrational world, or a more highly developed sense of intuition. This sense of intuition is as essential to everyone for their general wellbeing, health, and success as a well developed bank account. It really is as simple as that. Without it we are depriving ourselves of one whole side of the story of life, of our lives.

There is only something magical or mystical or weird about information that is unfamiliar, incomplete, or unwieldy. Once we are adept at receiving and processing a wider range of information, the mystery is revealed to be what it is, an adjunct to the whole range of information that we use to support our lives every day of the week. Many people with strong Metal chi appear to be very astute or perceptive, enjoy great success in the business world, and seem to magically turn whatever they touch to gold. This alchemist's talent is simply the product of the attention they pay to their intuitive abilities.

So, how can you develop your own intuition?

1. Begin to be more aware of your body, of how it is feeling, of which parts need attention. Specifically, you should become aware of your body's needs at any one time to support your attempt to be increasingly healthy.

2. Increase the level of your consciousness by being more in touch with your senses. In order to do this you will certainly need to dispense with some of your array of "numbing out" devices.

3. Spend more time in, and pay more attention to, the natural world. This may mean noticing the change in the colors of the sky, the appearance of the moon, or simply walking into the garden or a park and noticing the way the plants and wildlife are changing daily. Begin to develop an ability to observe and sense and listen to your surroundings. Unexpected things happen, and you need to be able to be aware of it when they do.

4. Work on developing this ability to use all your senses to observe what is happening around you. Listen with absolute attention, until the moments after someone has stopped speaking. Watch how they hold their body, how they move, how their color changes, the pitch, tone, and quality of their voice alters, and be aware of what is happening to their breath as they are talking. Take this ability to be aware beyond human interaction, and begin to interact in this way with animals, plants, and the whole of your physical environment.

5. Extend this heightened awareness (it stops becoming hard work and becomes automatic very quickly) to every day and every place and every situation. Next, choose a day when you feel relaxed, healthy, and centered, suspend any remaining cynicism and assume an ability to second-guess your environment with absolute accuracy. Go out and begin to practice living intuitively and enjoy the difference it makes to your day.

Developing your Metal chi will enable you to feel the world around you with more than your five senses, your whole body will be alert and awake on all levels.

Mastering your Emotions

This heightened awareness that you can develop and enjoy in your life is partly the result of increased sensitivity to your surroundings. It is also the result of your increased willingness and capacity to participate more fully in the business of being alive. This is something that you are increasingly able to risk doing as your Earth chi is more supported and you can rely on your own resources to maintain you in a grounded and centered position. As this situation develops, the joy and the emotional pain quota will invariably rise, but so will your ability to move between emotions, experiencing a wider range and intensity. There are people walking around who have never been in love, never felt wonder, never felt ecstatically happy or deeply contented. Neither may they have felt truly afraid, deeply jealous, or absolutely enraged. It is a matter of choice.

If you choose to pursue a sensitive way of being, it is helpful to know that the ability to let go of that which is no longer useful is crucial in the business of being able to take more in, and feel more.

Too much pain experienced and inappropriately held onto can have a devastating effect on your health and wellbeing, as we all know only too well. In Chinese philosophy the lung function is seen as the seat of wisdom, because here lies the ability to absorb and assimilate useful matter while waste is eliminated. In every painful moment or situation there is a lesson to be learned. The greater the pain, the bigger the lesson. Once the information has been identified and the wisdom distilled from the situation, the memory of the event can be discarded. But it is very difficult to let go of the pain until the benefit has been identified. Your work must always be to search for the message in each moment of pain, thus reinterpreting the event to your benefit, and avoiding arriving at a situation where you are stuck with a negative emotion that becomes a habitual response in a whole range of other situations. If you ignore the initial moment of difficulty, as with physical pain, it is inevitable that a more powerful one will be right along behind it to draw your attention back to that place of need.

Letting go of past hurt is one of the great tasks we have before us if we are going to support our Metal chi, and all the physical and emotional systems that depend on it.

The way in which the memory of events and how you feel about them is stored in the body has a huge bearing on your ability to let them go and dissipates the impact that they could continue to have on you long after they constitute any real threat to your wellbeing.

One of the keys to forgiveness is the ability to learn and see the benefit in every situation. It seems that once you have acknowledged the full impact of a situation on you and felt the full range of feelings, however difficult, associated with it, then the only way forward is to take all this material you have gathered and put it to good use, partly to avoid having to repeat the lesson in a more powerful form. The other great incentive to learning and letting go is that you are less likely to perpetuate the syndrome of habitual response and acting from a position of damage which will inevitably pass the pain around and around among family and friends, or worse still transmit it to your children to either deal with or pass on to theirs.

Learning to let go of deep hurt is one way of mastering your emotions and ensuring that they are under your own control, no longer something to be avoided or even feared. It is also useful to know that if powerful emotion is not allowed to enter the body at a deep cellular level and sit there for lengthy periods of time it is much easier to recover from the effect of the initial impact and move on.

Emotions held deep in the body are sometimes very hard to shift using the power of the intellect alone. In my healing work I almost always work with the body and the mind together, and through your practice of yoga, as set out in this book, it will be possible for you to detoxify your body and mind of all that redundant material at a very deep level, although you may also wish to seek help. The way in which you breathe, particularly during times of stress, has a great impact on the way in which you can recover at a later date.

You breathe in very different ways in different situations, and the way in which you breathe is responsible for instructing your mind about how you should respond mentally to any situation. By altering your breath you can protect yourself from some of the escalating impact of events, and from the way the memory of events and their fallout is stored in the body.

The Breath of Life

For many people protecting themselves means building walls around themselves. When you trust Metal chi and open yourself up, the chi will protect you far more than those walls ever can.

Chinese thinking suggests that the lungs are responsible for producing defensive Wei Qui chi, a yang chi which circulates at the surface of the body protecting it against climatic or pathogenic forces. Balanced Metal chi, as indicated by the health, not only of the lungs themselves, but also of the skin, nose, sinuses, and elimination system, indicates a strong ability to protect oneself. This is different from avoiding life to protect oneself or starving oneself of life.

So what can you do to avoid arriving in this position? How can you go about remedying it if this is your current position? How can you build on your inner strength and natural defenses? For the answers to these questions

Hanging onto an increasingly ossified existence surrounded by a series of battlements erected to protect oneself from pain, (that almost certainly lies within and is only triggered by external sources), is evidence of Metal chi in a state of deep imbalance.

you need to return to the ideas introduced in the previous pages and look to the breath as a source of support and control. Here is a wonderfully practical way to support yourself and keep your body free from any potential disease that is being harbored in the form of redundant emotion.

Think for a moment about the way that you are breathing right now. Consider the capacity, breadth, and depth of the inhalation, the ability to hold the breath without struggle, the fluidity, control, and length of the exhalation, and the ability to accept the emptiness and stillness of no breath. Now remember how you breathe when you are suddenly startled, angry, or afraid.

Habitually, your response to certain emotions is reflected in your breath. The normal response to fear is to place emphasis on the inhalation; to be angry is to become ragged for the whole cycle; to be anxious is for the inhalation to become shallow and the exhalation weak; to be depressed is for the exhalation to dominate; to be fearful is to minimize the level of the whole cycle, as if hiding and trying to suppress the breath altogether.

*

Breathe deep and sure and you will be strengthened by the chi around you.

Breath and Visualization

Breathing is food for the soul, it is through this that we connect most clearly with the universal chi. Sitting still and breathing slowly and calmly will bring you closer to the world around you.

If you can come to understand your habitual breathing patterns, you can learn a lot about what emotions have become entrenched. You can also choose to change this habitual pattern and the emotional mind-set that it represents. At times of anger you can choose to breathe smoothly and freely if you want to become calm. When you are afraid or anxious you can consciously broaden and deepen your whole breathing cycle signaling to yourself that you are safe. When you are depressed you can allow a fuller inhalation to stimulate your chi and help you to access the emotions hidden within the depressed behavior. At moments of hurt, when you feel under attack, or when old emotional patterns are threatening to take control of the current situation, you can get back into the "Now" by using a deliberately centered way of breathing, which will quickly bring you into an alert but grounded state. This way of breathing is the one that you will have become used to from your yoga practice—breathing in through the nose, visualizing the bridge of the nose to be very broad and the whole nasal cavity to be clear and wide, and then allowing the breath to leave the body through a relaxed mouth, with the jaw soft and the tongue easy in the mouth. By refusing to choose to tense the body around stress-signaling breathing patterns, it is possible to stay in control of the response that you have in any situation. If an extreme response like fear or rage is necessary, then it will be experienced in the most effective and usable way.

It has been my experience that our breath is fundamental to keeping our emotional life fluid and developing. Because so much of the way the body is held is dependent on the breath (everything from the torso to the position of the neck, the face, the arms is immediately affected), the breathing habits will exacerbate any holding of emotions within the body. If you can work with the body and the breath and the emotions simultaneously, then you will get real results.

I have found it very useful to combine visualization with breathing exercises, using the power of the intellect to assist the process of accepting newness and letting go of old attachments. One very simple and useful exercise is to visualize yourself seated at the edge of a beautiful, serene, and bountiful ocean. Feel the warm sand supporting your body and the sweet air drifting down from the heavens to bathe your body and soul. As you sit, feel the first wave that comes to meet you bringing a flow of newness and air into your body and filling it with peace. As the wave recedes allow it to pull from your body all the air of staleness and old attachment that you have been long wishing to let go, and allow yourself to exhale deeply and fully. A time of emptiness and wonder follows, before the next wave of newness begins to approach and the cycle begins again.

Sit for some time listening to the sound of the sea, feeling the peace and breathing with the waves. Allow the sea to gratefully receive all that you no longer need. From its great and limitless abundance it will both renew and replenish you.

Food
Food and Emotions

*

*Try eating food in a
calm unhurried way—
eat slowly, savoring
every mouthful and
turn food into a meal
full of pleasure.*

Regardless of the amount or quality of food that you consume, it will not energize the body if your breathing is insufficient. It is the combination of the lung chi dropping down through the body and the way it combines with the functioning of the other elements (in particular Earth chi, which governs digestion and assimilation), that gives rise to the assimilation and absorption of the food you eat. Therefore it is not enough to open your mouth, chew, and swallow to ensure that you are benefiting from the food that you are eating.

This is one of the reasons why it is important to be aware of the emotional and physical state that you are in while you are eating. Obviously, if you eat when your breath is agitated by an excess of emotion that you are in the middle of expressing or processing, then the food will do different things to your body than if you had eaten that same food when you were feeling relaxed. A person who is not at ease with the flow of their emotions and regularly eats while at their mercy, (or worse still, in an attempt to try and control or dull them), will find that all sorts of problems will arise for them connected to poor digestion, absorption, assimilation, or elimination of their food. This is because of the connection between lung chi and Earth chi.

Furthermore, undergoing a period of stress, emotional or physical, will often cause a series of allergic reactions to food that has been happily eaten before. The allergy is likely to recede and eventually disappear once the whole elemental balance of the body has been reset. Allergies are a defense mechanism used by the body to guide you back onto the path of feeding it in a way that it needs to be fed. Eliminating suspected foods and carrying on without making any other changes may help in the short term, but you will need to go through a more complete and thorough transformation to restore the body in the long term.

One of the things you can do to help your body to be able to accept and make good use of the food you eat is to work with your awareness of your breath and your ability to be conscious of its link with emotions and physical processes. Carrying this awareness through to times when you eat, and choosing not to eat when you are particularly caught up in your emotions can be a powerful way to begin to support your body, creating health for body, mind, and soul.

The Yin and Yang of Food

In the same way that Metal chi drops down through the body, nurturing it at the deepest level and supporting your ability to absorb nourishment from the food that you eat, Earth chi is needed to support Metal chi and lung function. One of the fundamental ways to support the breath and eliminate problems such as asthma, is to sort out eating patterns and adjust what you are eating. Yang food will be more energetically

Understanding that food can be more or less yin or yang is a very useful tool when you are trying to adjust the content, cooking style, and manner of eating.

To eat to boost your chi, you need to combine yin and yang foods to create nourishment for your soul as well as your body.

compact, dense, solid, or intense in its make-up, smell, or taste. Yin food will be more dispersed, cooler, and passive in its energetic content and the way that it is received. If you understand these differences then you can start to make eating choices along the lines of needing Yinising or Yangising. To eat a bowl of salad greens and a clear vegetable soup, for example, would be to eat a yin meal, while a plateful of sausage, carrots, and baked potato would be yang. A cookie and a glass of milk would be a more yang snack than an ice cream or a strawberry mousse. Things cooked for a long time in a contained space (inside an oven, in a pot

secured with a lid) will be more yang than things cooked for a short time in an open pot, or eaten raw.

Two raw foods will be more or less yin, for example a carrot is less yin than some lettuce.

It is particularly important to achieve a balance between yin and yang in your eating if you want to support your lung chi. The temptation to survive on a diet of very yang food will not support your need to breathe with fluidity, or your need to eliminate toxins from your body with that same ease. Eating large amounts of baked wheat products in particular, or hard dry snack foods will not support your Metal chi, nor will eating overcooked or burned food, or food cooked by someone who is rushed or angry. I find it useful to temper the consumption of these foods with the nourishing yang foods such as root vegetables cooked long and slow, warming, gently spiced, and aromatic soups, good quality grains and above all simple combinations of foods. It is obviously good to enjoy a variety of foods, but this is not the same thing as eating complicated meals. Eating meals which are complicated in terms of content or cooking process invariably becomes a substitute for cooking with a variety of vibrant, pure ingredients in a straightforward fashion.

Keep your cooking simple, with wholesome natural ingredients. The combination of simple dishes eaten in a relaxed way encourages the vibrancy of Metal chi.

Food and Energy Exchange

If you have followed all the advice about eating in this book, and all that you have heard, read, and variously imbibed over the years from all the other myriad sources, and you are still experiencing problems connected to eating, digestion, or maybe your weight, there is one more thing to consider.

This is the issue of taking energy from food, and food being used as a way of passing energy between people, not usually consciously, but in the same way that energy is passed between wearers of the same clothes, by sleeping in someone else's bed, or sitting in a chair that they have just vacated. This issue has been mentioned briefly earlier in this book, but deserves specific attention in this Metal chi section, because it has to do with susceptibility to what could be called vibrational, or psychic, energy.

As you develop your intuition and your awareness to energy of all kinds, you may also begin to notice that food acts as a form of currency or energy exchange. Eating food cooked by a person when they are almost fully occupied with one or another emotion (often connected to a specific event) can become a way of taking on that emotion for them and inadvertently helping them to process that emotion, or transmute that energy. Problems may arise when you are holding a surfeit of that emotion yourself, or when you are habitually channelling energy and are seen as a clear conduit or escape route for the held chi.

The experience in the body may be similar to an allergic reaction. It may be intense, dramatic, with a very swift onset. More often, it will manifest as a vague feeling of discomfort or disquiet. The trick to restoring your original good feeling is, as ever, to track back to the causal moment, the time and place of eating, to recognize your response as something beyond the purely physical, and deal with it on a purely energetic

Eating food cooked by a person when they are almost fully occupied with one or another emotion (often connected to a specific event) can become a way of taking on that emotion for them and inadvertently helping them to process that emotion, or transmute that energy.

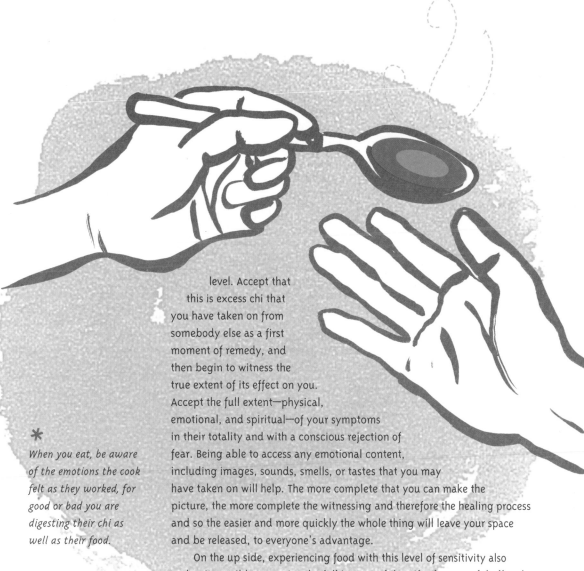

level. Accept that this is excess chi that you have taken on from somebody else as a first moment of remedy, and then begin to witness the true extent of its effect on you. Accept the full extent—physical, emotional, and spiritual—of your symptoms in their totality and with a conscious rejection of fear. Being able to access any emotional content, including images, sounds, smells, or tastes that you may have taken on will help. The more complete that you can make the picture, the more complete the witnessing and therefore the healing process and so the easier and more quickly the whole thing will leave your space and be released, to everyone's advantage.

On the up side, experiencing food with this level of sensitivity also makes it possible to receive the full impact of the gift of a spoonful offered from a loved one's plate or an fall-harvested fruit eaten in midwinter when you need some sunshine to fill your body and soul.

When you eat, be aware of the emotions the cook felt as they worked, for good or bad you are digesting their chi as well as their food.

Index

Acknowledgments

I would like to thank my husband Rob and my children Alexei, Josef, and Imogen whose support and example made the creation of this book possible.

I would also like to thank Ariel Warner (OE) and Roberta Shewen (Mariella) for the channeling and healing they facilitated in Carnac, France prior to its writing. Sue Morfew deserves recognition for her role as Yoga teacher and woman extraordinaire. Gavin Livingstone and Shiv are to be acknowledged for recognizing me and thereby allowing all the rest to come to pass. All the students and clients of the Feng Shui Foundation (past and present) are also acknowledged and thanked for their significant contribution to my work. I thank from the bottom of my heart the Shamans who come out to me when I am working and they are needed, and because of whom I am here to tell the tale. In particular Gavin, Mariella, Brooke, Katherine, Nigel, Don, Joyce, Veronica, and Nyat.

Bibliography

The Feng Shui Handbook
Master Lam Kam Chuen
Gaia, 1995

Traditional Acupuncture:
    The Law of the Five Elements
Dianne M. Connelly
The Center for Traditional
    Acupuncture, 1975

I Ching
Stephen L. Karcher & Rudolph
    Ritsema
Element Books, 1994

Clear Your Clutter with Feng Shui
Karen Kingston
Piatkus, 1998

Creating Sacred Space with Feng
    Shui
Karen Kingston
Piatkus, 1996

Nine Star Ki
Mishio Kushi
One Peaceful World, 1991

Sacred Space Clearing and
    Enhancing the Energy of Your
    Home
Denise Linn
Rider, 1995

Feng Shui Astrology
Jan Sandifer
Piatkus, 1997

The Living Earth Manual
Stephen Skinner
Arkana, 1989

Feng Shui Made Easy
William Spear
Throsons, 1995

Tao Te Ching
Lao Tsu
Wildwood House Ltd., 1992

The I Ching or Book of Changes
Richard Wilhelm (trans.)
Routledge and Kegan Paul, 1968

The Illustrated I Ching
R. L. Wing
HarperCollins, 1987

The Ki
Takashi Yoshikawa
St Martin's Press, 1986

The Feng Shui Directory
Jane Butler-Biggs
Watson-Guptill, 2000

Feng Shui in 10 Simple Lessons
Jane Butler-Biggs
Watson-Guptill, 1999

Feng Shui Journey
Jon Sandifer
Piatkus, 2000

The Prophet
Kahil Gibran
Phoenix Press, 1986

Useful Addresses

UK

Feng Shui Foundation
The Spinney 59 Wickham Hill
Hurstpierpoint
West Sussex
BN6 9NR
England
For Feng Shui Consultations, Space
     Clearing , Shamanic healing,
     and Yoga.

Feng Shui Store
2 Douglas Road
Aylesbury
Bucks
HP20 IHW
T/F: 01296 399100
www.fengshuiweb.co.uk

Feng Shui Academy
Waterside
PO Box 60
Buxton
SK17 7FH
T: 07071 22 80 80
F: 01298 73882
www.fengshuiacademy.co.uk

Feng Shui Society
377 Edgware Road
London
W2 1BT
T: 07050 289 2000
www.fengshuisociety.org.uk

America

Feng Shui Directory of Consultants
PO Box 6701
Charlottesville
VA 22906
www.fengshuidirectory.com

American Feng Shui Institute
108 North Ynez Avenue
Suite 202
Monterey Park
CA 91754
T: 626 571 2757
F: 626 571 2065
www.amfengshui.com

International Feng Shui Guild
Sacred Spaces
784 E. Homestead Drive
Highlands Ranch
CO 80126

Feng Shui Designs Inc.
PO Box 399
Nevada City
CA 95959
T/F: 1 800 551 2482
www.fsdi.com

Canada

Canadian Feng Shui Centre
1465 Dewbourne Crescent
Burlinton
Ontario L7M IE8
www.fengshui.ca

Australasia

Feng Shui Design Studio
PO Box 7788 Bondi Beach
Sydney 2026
Australia
T: 61 2 9365 7877
F: 61 2 9365 7847

Feng Shui Consultants
PO Box 34160
Birkenhead
Aukland
New Zealand
T: 64 9 483 7513